A THEOLOGY FOR MINISTRY

A THEOLOGY FOR MINISTRY

Creating Something of Beauty

Gordon E. Jackson

St. Louis, Missouri

© Copyright 1998 by Gordon E. Jackson

All rights reserved. No part of this book may be reproduced without written permission from Chalice Press, P.O. Box 179, St. Louis, MO 63166-0179.

All scripture quotations, unless otherwise indicated, are from the *New Revised Standard Version Bible,* copyright 1989, Division of Christian Education of the National Council of the Churches of Christ in the USA. Used by permission.

Cover design: Lynne Condellone

Interior design: Elizabeth Wright

This book is printed on acid-free, recycled paper.

Visit Chalice Press on the World Wide Web at
www.chalicepress.com

10 9 8 7 6 5 4 3 2 1   98 99 00 01 02 03

Library of Congress Cataloging-in-Publication Data

Jackson, Gordon R.
   A theology for ministry: creating something of beauty / by Gordon R. Jackson.
      p. cm.
   Includes bibliographical references.
   ISBN 0-8272-3634-4
    1. Process theology.   2 Theology, Practical.   3. Aesthetics—Religious aspects—Christianity.   I. Title.
BT83.6.J33   1998   98-37327
230'.046—dc21   CIP

Printed in the United States of America

To all the people
with whom I counseled
over the years

Table of Contents

	Foreword John B. Cobb, Jr.	ix
	Preface	xiii
1	A Process Metaphysical Framework	1
2	The Past Massively Present	10
3	Divine Love As Persuasive Power	29
4	Shalom: Gift and Actualization	39
5	Importance	52
6	Intentionality	63
7	Imagination	76
8	Linguistic Expression	89
9	Spirituality: The Thing of Beauty	101

Foreword

Gordon Jackson has given us process theology in a new key. The older process theologies have accented Whitehead's or Hartshorne's doctrine of God, emphasizing God's responsiveness to the world against traditional assertions of God's impassibility, and emphasizing God's persuasive power against traditional assertions of God's omnipotent control of all that happens. Jackson knows, accepts, and utilizes this work.

Some of these older theologies have also dealt with other central traditional doctrines such as sin and redemption, Christ, the church, and eschatology. Nothing in Jackson's presentation discounts this kind of theological work. But his focus is different.

Jackson has drawn forth central ideas of Whitehead that are not, on the surface, so obviously theological. He organizes his presentation around such themes as the massiveness of the past, persuasive power, peace, importance, and imagination. This culminates in a discussion of spirituality as the attainment of beauty.

The beauty that is attained by spirituality is, of course, primarily the beauty of the soul. This is a crucial emphasis of Whitehead, but one that is often misunderstood. Beauty is so often identified with the beauty of nature and art objects that to give beauty the central place it has in both Whitehead and Jackson seems wrong to most Christians. We usually make the ethical central, not the aesthetic. Indeed, especially we Protestants have had difficulty giving the aesthetic an important role in our faith.

One of Jackson's main contributions is to pervade his whole book with the sense of the importance of beauty. The beauty of art and nature contributes to the beauty of the soul's life, but so do righteousness and justice. Openness to the needs and joys of others contributes even more. The spirituality of beauty enables us to affirm the role of ethics without losing deep appreciation for the fact that the life of faith far transcends the sphere of morality as usually understood.

Jackson calls his book a theology for ministry. It would be unfortunate if that were read as meaning that it is only for pastors. Certainly pastors can benefit richly from reading it. But it is written for all who minister, and that means for all Christians.

Indeed, there are many of other religious communities, and those of no religious community at all, who still minister to one another. Although the book is written by a Christian for Christians, and this is clear in his language and some of the sources he cites, the "theology" it offers can be adapted still more broadly. The past weighs heavily on all, not just Christians, and the questions of importance and imagination are universal human ones. The hunger for an authentic spirituality, to which the book speaks, is widespread in our culture.

Jackson has long taught pastoral care and counseling. His sensitive concern for real human beings in the complexity of their actual situations provides a background for all these chapters. He draws on psychological literature as well as theology and philosophy and the analysis of culture. He does not impose Whitehead's themes, but allows them to grow out of insightful discussion of the human condition.

Because Jackson knows that he is drawing heavily on the thought of Whitehead, he begins by explaining the overall structure of Whitehead's thought. He does so lucidly and accessibly, and the reader of the other chapters will certainly benefit from studying this introduction.

One's appreciation for most of what he writes in subsequent chapters does not depend on any prior knowledge of Whitehead or even on the introduction Jackson offers. Indeed, one need not be able to identify where Whitehead's influence appears in order to appreciate the ideas. On the other hand, thoughtful readers will know a lot about Whitehead's thought by the time they finish this book.

Process thinkers owe Jackson a debt for expanding and deepening the meaning of process theology. All who would minister owe him a debt for expanding the horizons of ministry and for sharing his wisdom about that ministry. As you turn to the text, prepare for a feast.

John B. Cobb, Jr.
Claremont, California
September 25, 1998

Preface

This book is intended for the total ministry of the church: professional clergy and every lay member. In fact, *laity* comes from the Greek meaning "a people," "a nation," "a multitude." The church is the "body of Christ," a spiritual reality or spiritual community, which centers in Christ and takes its marching orders from Christ. All members of this Christian community are ministers, called to fulfill the commandment of love in the world. For all these ministers this book is intended. Much of its contents may seem to be more directed to the professional clergy, and this is due to their special responsibility to equip themselves, to be sure, but especially to equip all other members of the church to fulfill their ministry. But in these pages ministry is the ministry of all the people of God who are called by God to be servants working with the Holy Spirit to build the kingdom of God.

My vision of that ministry is an aesthetic vision: *to work with the creating and recreating God to create something of beauty in each moment of living,* both in each individual life and in corporate living. A primary example of that ministry is the Stephen Ministry, so deeply engaged in the practice of loving service, guided by the cosmic Artist who is ceaselessly laboring to create souls of beauty. God labors in the context of a vast past forming all of us and a rich future of possibilities informing all of us, to help each church member to actualize himself or herself toward a richer spiritual fulfillment and to practice servanthood or ministry more effectively. This book attempts to describe the massive past, the lure of possibilities, and the existential actualizing of past and possibilities into a moment of becoming.

To enable us to picture this momentous movement of time under the direction of the cosmic Artist, I am employing a twentieth-century philosophy and theology called process thought. My intention is to bring a vision for ministry to suggest what souls of beauty look like and how they might participate more intentionally in ministry with God to create something of beauty as shalom with its peace, harmony, and wholeness in the world around them. I see ministry as creating something of beauty under the persuasive artistry of God in lives each of us touches: family, friends, neighbors, fellow workers, strangers along the way.

The opening chapters I acknowledge to be somewhat heavy. But it is necessary to take a detailed look at the massive past that informs every person—the one ministering, and the one to whom ministry in whatever form is being offered. Each person, whether in the pulpit, or the pew, or the house next door, or the adjacent office desk, or a mile down the road, is never just the person we see or hear. That person is deeply embedded in his or her past, of which neither she nor he is very conscious. In order to be ministers we need to have some sense of the massive past informing our very beings. And the future, crowded with possibilities, a future constantly beckoning us, is also largely unknown to the person to whom ministry is turned as well as to the ministering one.

The one true God, knowing each iota of every past and the possibilities relevant to each person's past, is the co-creator along with that person of each present moment. Therefore, I have employed a process model in the opening chapters to elaborate on the massive past and the infinitude of possibilities in order to picture God's gracious functioning in every instant of becoming—for *each* moment of becoming is the context in which ministry functions. And ministry is the servant role of all the people of God working with God to create something of beauty, that is, a spirituality that results when the divine Spirit and the human spirit come into an organismic rendezvous that can flower in a new human being, a fresh creation, a new birth of personhood.

To strive toward such ministry we need to appreciate the meaning of *importance*, for we are always in the process of deciding, and our decisions depend on what we regard as important. But we cannot deal with what is really important without understanding the place of *intentionality*, for in essence it is our aim into the future, our intentions, that bear directly on our commitments—for instance, to make love our aim, as Paul urged the people of Corinth to do. But to focus on importance and intentionality we need to lift up *imagination*, for we are all image-makers, and our images are essential to all communication. The Bible is wonderfully laden with images—for example, the shepherd imaging God, water imaging cleansing and renewal in baptism, the cross imaging the cost of forgiveness. But without *language*, which is a fundamental mode of our very being, we cannot express ourselves in ways that are pivotal in every form of ministry. So importance, intentionality, imagination, and linguistic expression are essential chapters to help us toward our own second-by-second becoming, as well as our becoming better ministers. Then, perhaps, all of us who are the people of God, the congregation of God's people, can work more in harmony with God, the cosmic Artist, to create something of beauty—a deeper spirituality of love, peace, and joy in ourselves and others.

To that aesthetic end this book is dedicated. I am profoundly grateful to John B. Cobb, Jr., and to Arthur Peterson for their careful reading of this manuscript and for their incisive and creatively helpful comments. I need also to express my deep gratitude to Karen Kadel, the perceptive and meticulous person that she is, for her caring work in transcribing my miserable handwriting into typed copy.

An Addendum

The original title for this book was *The Church's Ministry: Creating Something of Beauty*. The editor of Chalice Press, David P. Polk, correctly found the title to be too limiting and suggested *A Theology for Ministry: Creating Something of Beauty*. The church's ministry would too often focus on professional ministry: rabbi, priest, pastor, or whatever title of the professional minister. He or she is included, of course, in the term ministry. But numerically that would be a very small inclusion. The term "minister" includes the total laity, the people of God, ministering by sharing God's steadfast love in the total context in which they live, and move, and have their being. The context is all-inclusive: with family, fellow workers, neighbors, the congregation, racially different people, the aging lonely at home alone or in nursing homes, children with special needs, adolescents alone on the streets or in gangs, people living in poverty, every human being for whom God's encompassing love is intended. And that love requires a servant people to minister God's redemptive grace.

The contents of this book are the theological attempts to locate the structure and function of God's servant people in an organismic framework that sees all of existence in a processive mode of becoming, realizing, and contributing. Each of us is summoned by the creative God at work in the world to work with the divine Artist, borrowing from Alfred North Whitehead, the father of process philosophy, to create something of beauty as we process through our days and years empowered by the creative love of God to bring healing to our communal life.

1

A Process Metaphysical Framework

Christianity is a religion seeking a metaphysic.
Alfred North Whitehead

The Judeo-Christian faith is the story of divine-human encounters over centuries culminating in Jesus Christ, the Word made flesh. The human response is faith responding to the grace of God: faith that is trust, commitment, and belief.[1] Trust is viscerally settling down into everlasting Arms as an infant settles into its mother's cradling arms, a paradigm described by Erik H. Erikson as basic trust vs. mistrust. Commitment is the role of the will, pitching one's life toward the God in whom one trusts. This is the "intention of faith," as Martin Buber has emphasized, the soul projected toward that which is of ultimate worth and is therefore worshipful. Belief emerges from trust and commitment and is a reflection upon them. It is the mind's search for meaning, which in Paul Tillich's analysis is an ontological need. In Anselm's famous dictum, faith seeks understanding, and belief, which is theological in nature, is this seeking.

This theological search cannot be insulated from the rest of life's experience. Ours is a connectional world, and theology is the effort to see how the human experience of God connects with everyday existence, with the realities of the various sciences, with the entirety of creation. It is the search to understand evil and to develop an ethical system to help us achieve some better order. It is the search for language for the sake of communication and for the structure and meaning of community made possible by language.

Theologians have employed various frameworks with which to explicate their understanding of God, of God's relationship to the whole of creation, and the creation's ways of knowing, ways of working, ways of behaving. Augustine used a neoplatonic perspective. Aquinas employed the principles of Aristotle. The framework I am proposing as a matrix for seeing how all the interconnections of existence operate—from God to subatomic structures—is the metaphysical vision of Alfred North Whitehead, British/American mathematician, scientist, and philosopher.

In this opening chapter my intention is to employ a generalized description of how reality looks from the past through the present into the future. Though these terms have a temporal ring, we are not conceiving time in the way a watch or a calendar measures time. That spatializes time, dividing it up into segments—which is necessary, of course, for human living. Rather, time in this philosophical perspective is *duration*, which means that the past is a continuity into the present and endures into every succeeding present.[2] There are *the massive past, the future replete with possibilities, and the present actualizing itself as it faces both past and future.* This is a processive or organismic vision that sees every iota of stuff in the universe as interrelated, and sees God as the ultimately related One.

Without getting too deeply into the intricacies of process thought, we need to look at three realities that can help us locate ourselves in each "moment" of becoming. This is not a time-measured "moment" of some determinate length but the individual's creating itself out of its past and out of the possibilities relevant to it. The actualizing occasion is where the past and future meet, and in this meeting a unique selfhood is created. As Whitehead put it, "A new creation has to arise from the actual world [the past] as much as from pure potentiality [the future]: it arises from the total universe."³

The Past as Actuality

We begin with the actual world. This is the world that has been actualized, that has come into being. It is the massive stuff of the past, near and distant. (We will detail this past in the next chapter.) The past consists of millions upon millions of years that are with us yet, as well as the hundredth of a second ago that began with the subject of this sentence (whether for the writer or for the reader).

Take a feeling of anger. A fraction of a second ago, let us say, I felt anger. That feeling of anger ties in with perhaps millions of previous feelings of anger spread throughout my life. And they tie in with the threat of danger lodged in my reptilian brain which we shall examine in chapter 2, a threat that may have produced angry aggressive behavior within our reptilian ancestors. This past is the environment of completed actions. Once each of those actions was a stage of incompleteness, which is what the present is. They were struggling for determination, to become actual, to put themselves together in a decided or finished way. Once they actualized themselves they became past. They perished as self-aware moments coming into actuality. But they did not cease to be. They are now beings or realities or actualities in the past tense.

Perhaps it was a teenage moment walking in a Seattle fog at night. That was long ago. Yet that moment is with me still, part of the given that shapes me ever so silently from unconscious levels. My present moment, perhaps driving in the fog, or perhaps inundated with a sense of being lost, or perhaps in a moment of intellectual confusion, has as its antecedent the objective content of my walk in the fog.

Whitehead calls <u>this massive environment that is the past causal efficacy</u>,[4] for it is the efficient causation for each new moment of becoming. <u>We each have feelings that conform to the past</u>. That is, we keep grasping at deeper levels than consciousness for all that has preceded us. But this grasping is not a mental activity; it is feeling, physical feeling. We feel the past with our bodies. <u>We bring the past into the present by way of emotionally laying hold of</u> it. This is how the objective content of the past transforms into subjective feelings in the present. The present houses the past by conforming to it at sheer feeling level.[5]

Thus the past is objectively present. The past has lost its vivid sense of aliveness, but it has not lost its causative power for each successive moment. As a moment of experiencing, the past has had its day and ceases to be. But as a moment to be experienced, it is objectively present as part of the given, the stuff of life, which must be reckoned with. It has become data for all the successor moments in their tenths or thousandths of a second of becoming. <u>Thus the past has achieved *objective immortality*</u>; that is, it is available for each new moment of becoming. In Whitehead's words, <u>the "real antecedent world"</u> is the "objective content" for each new occurring moment. As the new moment begins, there "is nothing there apart from the real agency of the actual past, exercising its function of objective immortality."[6] The past is immanent in the present, participating in each new becoming. "The data for any one pulsation of actuality consists of the full content of the antecedent universe as it exists in relevance to that pulsation."[7]

It is almost frightening to realize that this is not merely my personal past, remembered and unremembered. This is the total past of all reality, the totality of the trillions of moments of natural/human history that are the environment massively present to each new moment arising out of that past. Each new moment actualizes itself out of the innumerable moments that once were struggling, became actual, and are now what we call past. The past is constitutive of each new moment as that arising moment conforms to, takes into itself, something of that past. This would amount to sheer determinism, a total repetition of the past, were it not for the equally profound role of the *future*.

The Future as Potentiality

The potential world is the future, a future crowded with possibilities, infinite in number. These possibilities—*eternal objects* in Whitehead's terms—are not actual as is the past. But they are to be actualized in each present. It is the realm of possibilities that give to each moment of experiencing the adventure that keeps life from being stale, repetitive, stereotypical. But it is this realm that confronts each moment with the necessity for deciding: this possibility or that, this shade of color or that, this turn in the road or that, the choice of this word or another, the taking of a friend's question in this way or that, the aim toward siding with the neighbor or passing by on the other side. In fact, most of the decisions are not either/or, but shades of differences. It is the realm of possibilities that introduces novelty into every deciding moment: to wear this dress, or take in that show, or step on this patch of ground, or participate in a flirtation, or sulk, or entertain the thought of relief through suicide. These are decisions between what the actualized past brings to each moment and what the potential future offers. These are also gross, obvious decisions. Most of our fraction-of-a-second to fraction-of-a-second deciding is *directionality*; that is, aiming our lives toward what Heidegger calls authentic or inauthentic existence, with myriad fluctuations between these two routes of becoming.

And yet all of this future orienting is only a very abstract way of expressing the future. Possibilities have no life in and of themselves. They are abstract potentials, such as blueness, or roundness, or hardness, or beauty, or ugliness, or orderliness. They are inert. Yet possibilities are there...but where? They are located in the eternal nature of God. They have a home in the conceptual or primordial being of God—fulfilling the ontological principle that "everything must be somewhere."[8]

It is God who knows the total past and who knows all possibilities, and this knowledge constitutes the omniscience of God. God is the agent in the universe who brings to bear upon each emerging moment just that possibility or grouping of possibilities relevant to it, since God knows the route of causal efficacy informing that moment. There is the past; there are the possibilities; and there is this emerging moment out of the past toward a new becoming. God gives direction to that self-actualizing moment. This is God as the principle of concretion, the divine persuader, luring the becoming entity in the midst of the vast environment that is informing it. God becomes the divine appetition trying gently to shape the becoming of each and every moment. Whitehead writes of God as the "poet of the world, with tender patience leading by his vision of truth, beauty, and goodness."[9] This is the "love of God for the world. It is the particular providence for particular occasions."[10] (We shall be returning to this interpretation of God in chapter 3.)

At the moment we are concentrating on how God, who houses all potentiality, and who knows fully and directly all the past, is a major player in the process of every self-realization. I am an aging white male of western roots. Already my possibilities are limited by age, color, gender, geography, culture. By empathy I can identify somewhat with a teenager, a black person, a female, an Asiatic. But the limitations are decidedly there. Within those limitations God's creative working challenges me with new possibilities to produce a moment of novelty in the present instant of my becoming. God is a major player; I am a major player too. Between massive past and relevant possibility, God does what God can to shape my aim for what I can or will become. And this takes us to the principle of *concrescence*.

The Present as Concrescing

Concrescence means growing together. That is what every present moment is all about: growing itself together out of all that the past offers it and all that relevant possibilities beckon it to become. But as we have seen, possibilities are a way of talking about God. It is God, who envisages all possibilities, who aims the best possibility upon the present moment. In Whitehead's language this is God's "initial aim" or "lure" for each actualizing moment. In biblical language it is the Word of God. It is God communicating the divine vision for what is the best in this concrete moment of becoming. This is the will of God for that tenth of a second of becoming.

Between the insistent past and God's vision or will for what is best, the concrescing moment must "decide" what it will become (its own aim) and put itself together, for better or for worse. Here enters faith as obedience, sin as disobedience, to the divine vision—for the concrescing moment's aim might be somewhat congruent with God's aim, or in opposition to it. But aim it will, and that aim is its own final cause since it guides the becoming of the emerging entity. Most of the time we are not consciously aware of any divine guiding, or even that we are in the throes of deciding toward a bit of novelty by way of possibilities looming before us. As with Jacob of old, we sometimes awake from our slumbers sensing, "Surely the Lord is in this place—and I did not know it" (Genesis 28:16).

The present—though a specious present because it is moving, becoming—is a "process of feelings," struggling out of two environmental directions (what the past offers out of what is, and what the future offers out of what may be) to add itself to reality in a form of novelty (and not mere repetition), thanks to the relevant possibilities God brings to it. Thus, the many become one and a new one creates itself to add to the many. God, who knows the total past totally and the realm of possibilities absolutely—and who is in the struggling occasioning moment empathically—brings the divine vision to bear upon the concrescing occasion for what is best, given that impasse.

The present is a bottleneck of time, a focusing of past actuality and future possibility, in which the arising new entity determines itself, deciding what it will become. And what it becomes in its awesome moment of bringing to birth a new event in its own and the world's history, it becomes for all subsequent others. For in becoming a new one out of the infinitude of the many, it instantaneously moves from subjective experiencing to objective actuality. It *is* through *experiencing;* now it is there as part of an enlarged past, enlarged because it has contributed itself to that past. Now it has become a new datum for the next "moment" of becoming and for the becoming of all future moments which will go through the identical process it has just completed. The magnum opus of Whitehead, *Process and Reality*, is entitled precisely: Reality follows upon process; process is creative of reality. Through the process of self-actualizing, reality is formed.

The actual occasion, or to use the gerund, the actual occasioning in each moment, is richly analyzed by Whitehead. But perhaps Heidegger's *Dasein*, the concrete human *being there* in its existential moment, can add to this richness of Whitehead's existential moment, the actual occasioning of each entity. I am proposing that the concrescence in process thought can be enriched by Heidegger's notion of mood as dread and the primordial structure of Dasein as care. For example, "dread" as a basic instance of mood in Heidegger as well as in Kierkegaard grounds the actual occasion in its moment of freedom as it faces potentiality. We feel threat—not fear of something definite, but angst as we are on the edge looking into the abyss of freedom with its indefiniteness.[11] Thus, dread or angst is part of each moment as that moment is deciding what it will become, guided by its aim in response to God's aim for it. The mood of dread may help us to sense what actual occasioning is going through, sometimes a quite painful process. Care in Heidegger is the primordial structure of Dasein. "Care is always concern and solicitude."[12] It undergirds willing; it is the concern toward potentiality. Caring would have direct bearing on the subjective aim of the actual occasion in Whitehead's metaphysical vision. In fact, Whitehead employs the Quaker use of "concern," whereby the "occasion as subject has a 'concern' for the object" which immediately "places the object as a component in the experience of the subject, with an affective tone drawn from this object and directed towards it. With this interpretation the subject-object relation is the fundamental structure of experience."[13] Both mood as dread and the basic concept of care in Heidegger's phenomenology suggest the power of stirring emotion resident in each soul's concrescing, often a wrenching struggle, filled with pathos, in its momentary becomings.

Each self is a society of occasions reaching backward to a massive past and forward to an infinity of possibilities. God reaches to the self to offer it the divine vision for its birth and growth toward novelty, a novelty value-laden because of God's dream for it then and there. Whitehead has pictured in nearly existential terms the emotions of the creative moment: "I find myself as essentially a unity of emotions, enjoyments, hopes, fears, regrets, valuations with alternatives, decisions—all of them subjective reactions to the environment as active in my nature."[14] We now turn to one part of that environment, the massive past, in considerable detail to underscore how massive it is.

2

The Past Massively Present

The present is saturated with the past and pregnant with the future.

Leibniz

A woman has just discovered that her husband is having an affair. She comes to see her pastor. A deacon in the church is obviously very anxious about his scheduled surgery the next morning. His pastor visits him in the hospital. <u>Who are these people?</u> Not their names, of course. Not their titles, ranks, vocations, or sundry other identifications self-selected or conferred by the society about them. Not simply the visible person sitting across from the pastor or lying in the hospital bed. Then who are they whom the pastor will try to help?

They are people buried like an iceberg in the North Atlantic, only a bit of them visible to the eye. Yet these people are seeking pastoral help from one equally submerged. The ocean in which their beings are so hidden is the depths of the past. It is a massive past buoying them up, permeating them with trillions of bits of information, only a trifle of which is consciously available to them. The pastor will try to help them and probably help them he or she will. The more informed the pastor is about the ocean depths the less likely will that pastor be like a blind man searching in a dark room for a black cat that isn't there, to borrow the cynic's perspective on philosophy.

This chapter is designed to help the pastor understand with what complexity pastoral care especially, but all forms of ministry, must work in helping hurting people cope with problems and crises. The oceanic past (which is that causally efficacious environment that we examined in chapter 1) is fed by numerous subterranean streams, four of which we shall look at briefly.

The Triune Brain

The human brain is made up of three parts, all very old. The brain stem, several hundred million years old, is the oldest and most primitive. It is located at the top of the spinal cord and includes the medulla, the pons, and the midbrain. It is this part of the brain that we share with lizards, reptiles, birds, and other mammals. Dr. Paul MacLean, Director of the Laboratory of Brain Evolution and Behavior of the National Institute of Mental Health, and a foremost researcher of the brain, has called the brain-stem the reptilian brain or the R-complex.[1]

The struggle for territory begins with the reptilian brain. The marking of boundaries with urine, the grinding of teeth, growling, and the erect genital are all symbols of aggressive display to ward off the stranger. Humans display a similar struggle for territory, marking boundaries of homesites, cities, states, nations, with fences, walls, no trespassing signs, and city limit signs. We claim space in such primitive ways as graffiti and carving initials on trees. Many wars are territorial in origin, coupling ethnic and racial identities with territorial needs and demands. Along with the struggle for territory is the struggle for dominance. Strutting, swaggering, chest thumping by the dominant male, the erect genital are aggressive displays in the primitive social pecking orders to establish authority as well as to ward off strangers. The obvious influence about strangers in our midst carries deep and tragic meaning for racial and ethnic divisions in human history and contemporary life. We have with us in the brain stem a long memory system with which we are still dealing. Our intolerance of, or discomfort in the presence of, blemishes may be related to strangeness, aggravating territorial needs and demands. As MacLean suggests, what are "physically, behaviorally, or ideologically regarded as blemishes, such as, for example, differences in color, race, ethnic forms of behavior, religious, and political beliefs," trace back to the R-complex. "An innate propensity to an abhorrence of blemishes would perhaps help to explain why, even in the absence of severe crowding, there are now so many ethnic and racial groups locked in prolonged and bloody struggle because of physical, religious, or ideological differences."[2]

MacLean suggests that the R-complex may well be the primordial location of the will-to-power that Nietzsche concluded is the basic life force of the entire universe.[3] With territorial protection and the struggle for dominance so basic, aggressivity is a very primitive desire, as Freud postulated under terms of the death instinct, but Freud had no inkling as to how deeply the aggressive drive is buried.[4]

Nor, of course, did Freud know the depths of the sex instinct, or as he preferred in his later writings, the life principle. For sex and courtship are part of the R-complex. This should not be surprising, for therein lies the propagation of all species. Again, as in aggressive behavior, bodily displays also serve courtship, often the same displays. For example, an erect genital can be either an aggressive display or a sexual display, depending on the situation.⁵ Freud's employment of the Id with its aggressive and sexual components coincides with the R-complex, suggesting how deep in the human brain are these two dominating drives, as Freud called them.⁶

Routinizing behavior is another linkage between humans and their brain ancestry by way of the R-complex. "Reptiles are slaves to routine, precedent, and ritual."⁷ Breaks in routine can cause fright and even panic among many animals. With humans stress becomes a factor, sometimes exceedingly serious, when meal times are not fulfilled, when day-to-day work is interrupted by a holiday, when ceremonial rituals are altered, as for example, Sunday morning programs of worship, or when a business meeting routine is interrupted. Fashions in dress and hair styles are imitated, a function of routinizing behavior. As William Barrett has written: "Habit and routine are great veils over our existence. As long as they are securely in place, we need not consider what life means; its meaning seems sufficiently incarnate in the triumph of the daily habit. When the social fabric is rent, however, man [sic] is suddenly thrust outside, away from the habits and norms he once accepted automatically."⁸

Compulsive and obsessive compulsive behavior, no stranger to the psychiatrist's office, involves the entire triune brain, of course, but has roots in the R-complex. As MacLean argues, "That part of the brain's intelligence that enforces routine has a powerful means, it seems, of making known when there has been a break in routine."⁹ Compulsive acts and ceremonial rituals help to preserve a semblance of routine and dissipate anxiety over the breakdown or changes in order. Routine is necessary for us to be able to concentrate on other demanding issues.

As we have seen, prosematic communication, that is, nonverbal, has its roots in the R-complex.¹⁰ We have cited socially communicative displays, for example, genital erection to warn trespassers, chest thumping by the dominant male, grinding of teeth, strutting, swaggering. Some of this sounds very familiar, especially arousing macho images of males in the human species.

While the human reptilian brain has enlarged through evolution perhaps as much as fourteen times,[11] it is not a mere relic of the past, but a very important part of the triune brain serving many continuing functions. We have with us in the brain stem a long memory system with which we are always dealing—for example, even partially human compulsive behavior in a memory system that goes back hundreds of millions of years. The R-complex is not a vestigial structure or a mere relic. Rather, it "plays an essential role in regulating the basic forms of behavior under consideration, including the control of the master routine and subroutines, as well as the four main kinds of prosematic [non-verbal] communication."[12] Richard Restak, in his excellent book *The Brain: The Last Frontier*, using a computer analogy, writes, "It seems reasonable to suppose that this ancient brain structure is contributing its own 'program' for influencing our behavior."[13] Borrowing from MacLean's research, Restak lists ritualism, awe for authority, social pecking orders, and even obsessive-compulsive neuroses as partially caused by our reptilian brain.[14] Our reptilian ancestors are very much with us in that small part of our brain which we have inherited from them.

The limbic system surrounds the R-complex. This system, which probably dates back 150 million years, includes the thalamus, hypothalamus, amygdala, pituitary, and hippocampus. The limbic part of the brain is an emotional control center. Hate, love, guilt, fear are all there. It is the area of the brain most concerned with emotion.[15] Xenophobia, which is an abnormal fear of strangers, may well center in the limbic system, notwithstanding that there is the threat of the stranger in the R-complex, thus suggesting how deeply rooted racism is. The stranger may be feared, hated, shunned, ostracized (banished to ghettos), killed. Restak quotes Edward O. Wilson, professor of zoology at the Museum of Comparative Zoology at Harvard University: "Value systems are probably influenced…by emotional responses programmed in the limbic system of the brain."[16]

The limbic system houses a relatively crude and primitive system of emotions, elaborating six basic and specific affects: desires (e.g., hunger, thirst, sex) anger, fear, dejection (e.g., sorrow, guilt, depression), joy, affection (sexual feelings and expression).[17] Karen Horney's universal need for affection would be located here.[18] This system houses emotional feelings that guide behavior necessary for self-preservation as well as preservation of the species.[19] For example, the separation cry, when the infant is lost or isolated, or is in any other kind of acute distress, is located here.[20] While the intellectual functions are in the neocortex, as we shall see, our affective behavior continues to be dominated by the relatively crude and primitive limbic system. To summarize in MacLean's words, "The limbic system is fundamentally involved in the experience and expression of emotion."[21]

The neocortex or cerebral cortex evolved perhaps tens of millions of years ago but accelerated greatly in dolphins and whales about twenty million years ago and took almost an emergent leap about 250,000 years ago in the evolution of the human brain of homo sapiens.[22] This human brain as we can call it is where both analytical and intuitive thinking take place and where human language is generated and learned communication has its home. MacLean believes that language originated with social needs, and so language helps to fulfill the need to communicate. Such social needs as instigating and developing language might be needed for cooperation among members of hunting bands, mother-infant relationships, the motivation to communicate to overcome separation, one of the most distressful of mammalian conditions.[23] Curiosity, abstract thinking, problem solving, anticipation, for example, of one's death as one's destiny, are the good as well as the painful fruits of the neocortex.[24] Very important to the human situation is that the neocortex is where information is received, processed, and remembered, where criticizing and reacting take place, and where willed action is primarily determined.[25]

The limbic and neocortex arouse each other. Thought (neocortex) arouses affects (limbic) and affections arouse thought. To be specific, the neocortex is related to the limbic system in such functions as parental care, play, the feelings and expressions of crying and laughter, which rank closely to language in reflecting the human condition, and social bonding, which may have favored the evolution of the human sense of empathy and altruism.[26] But it is in the neocortex that identification with the feelings of others is located, where empathy, including foresight and concern for the future of others, as well as the self, develops into an ability to stand outside of oneself, as it were, and enter the life of another. Here is probably the arising of conscience and the primarily human urge to create, the human being's perceiving and dealing with situations from intimate social involvement to the ever enlarging social milieu.[27] Finally, it is the neocortex where beliefs, as forms of rationality, take shape. "The limbic system has the capacity to generate out of context, affective feelings of conviction that we attach to our beliefs regardless of whether they are true or false."[28] It is the neocortex that modifies this in terms of more rationality, including countering the R-complex with its built-in rules for orderliness. The limbic system cannot come to believe in the reality, importance, and truth or falsity of an affective feeling. As MacLean puts it, "It is one thing to have a primitive illiterate mind for judging the authenticity of food or a mate, but where do we stand if we must depend on that same mind for beliefs in our ideas, concepts, and theories?"[29] Our limbic brain is imbued with emotion; our neocortex system is imbued with at least some rationality to help guide the emotion.

When we try to understand our triune brain, we may be tempted to see three brain parts, each of which is busily doing its thing. This is not the way the brain works. Rather, it is a process, with its three units interacting. As Restak says, "Mental activity thus takes on the quality of a dynamic process."[30] Our reasoning part of the brain, for example, reasons in tandem with emotions in the limbic and turf protection in the R-complex. There are constantly trodden pathways in the brain along which move neuronal impulses and chemicals informing the three parts of our brain. Neurons are the active agents in brain functioning sending messages throughout the R-complex, the limbic system, and the neocortex. Perhaps we can try to understand this processive movement throughout the brain system by imagining a church quarrel. The problem is that the young associate pastor has been working with some neighborhood kids who have motorcycles, some of whom are suspected of being on drugs, and all of whom seem socially and hygienically to be quite different from the middle-class aging congregation. The young pastor wants the church building opened two evenings a week for the "kids." He will be there with them and he will have a couple of volunteers from the church if he can get them or, if not, from the neighborhood. Some members think this is part of their congregation's ministry; others agree but think the building will be wrecked. Still others are utterly opposed to "these dirty, irresponsible school dropouts who have no interest in our church but only want to use it for their own wayward purposes. Our church will never be the same if we vote to let them in."

The triune brain is at work. The neocortex provides theological argument about the nature of the Church and its mission as it derives from its nature. That argument is countered with a specious rationalization from the doctrine of sin that when these kids repent, change their ways, clean up their act, they should be allowed to use the building, for then they will respect it. Both neocortex arguments are flooded with emotion from the limbic room adjacent to the neocortex. The argument from what the Church is all about is bathed with commitment fervor; and the specious attempt to invoke sin is equally charged because the rationalization is the desperate attempt to cover the fear these kids provoke with their motorcycles and their drugs, or at least their beer. The reptilian brain asserts its turf-keeping role, reminding all those within hearing that my grandfather helped build this church, and my family has been here for sixty years. I don't want these punks wrecking this place.

Reptilian aggressive turf keeping, limbic fear, hate, love, all intermeshed, and neocortex analysis based upon biblical and theological understanding and misunderstanding, mixed with some anticipatory anxiety, speed into neighboring brain parts. Back and forth the neurons race, millions upon millions of them, over the proposed use of the church building. Whatever the vote, some part of the brain will feel hurt. Enough hurts, uncared for, and the congregation is in deep trouble. Will the neocortex prevail? That is the hope. But Sagan reminds us: "The deep and ancient parts are functioning still."[31] But his hope is part of his realism: "The aperture to a bright future lies almost certainly through the full functioning of the neocortex—reason alloyed with intuition and with limbic and R-complex components, to be sure, but reason nonetheless: a courageous working through of the world as it really is."[32]

The Jungian Collective Unconscious

To continue with our metaphor of the iceberg, human consciousness is only the tip of the iceberg and our unconscious state is the whole of the iceberg hidden from view. Freud opened up the unconscious, but his tremendous insight was limited to the personal unconscious; that is, to the personal material each person represses into his or her unconscious. That was a rich insight in itself. Along came Jung, who deepened the concept of unconscious into the Collective Unconscious. Jung accepts the personal unconscious of Freud but sees it resting upon a deeper layer, "which does not derive from personal experience and is not a personal acquisition but is inborn." This Jung called the collective unconscious. It is not individual but universal, constituting a "common psychic substrate of a suprapersonal nature which is present in every one of us."[33]

The contents of the collective unconscious are the archetypes, which are universal, preexistent forms inherited by all individuals. Jung analyzed some of these archetypes, such as the Shadow, the Mother, Anima/Animus, Rebirth, the Child, the Hero, the Christ figure, and the Wise Old Man, among others.[34] These are primordial images, profound myths,[35] which motivate us powerfully without our being consciously aware even of their presence. A moment with the Anima archetype will reveal something of the archetype's power. The unconscious of a male contains a feminine element, as the unconscious of a female contains a male element (animus). The anima, or female element, in the male is a primordial image that emerges in a man's multiple contacts with women through his lifetime. Its value Jung pinpoints: "An inherited collective image of woman exists in a man's unconscious, with the help of which he apprehends the nature of woman."[36] No woman fulfills or even approximates this inherited anima. The anima first meets the mother; in some ways, therefore, mother is the most important woman in a man's life, because of this early, primitive archetypal connection with the woman. The male is inhabited by the opposite sex, to a point. *Anima* means "soul" and the female image plays a profound role in the definition of a male: his very soul is crucially female oriented. No individual woman fulfills this archetypal image; but the image projects itself on to every woman a male has contact with throughout his life. Men are not aware of this primordial image of female projecting on to each woman. But the image of woman so projected can be tragic. As Frieda Fordham has written, "Naturally this leads to endless misunderstanding, for most men are unaware that they are projecting their own inner picture of woman on to someone very different; most inexplicable love affairs and disastrous marriages arise in this way."[37] As Jung himself characterized the powerful anima-image: "Every mother and every beloved is forced to become the carrier and embodiment of this omnipresent and ageless image, which corresponds to the deepest reality in a man."[38]

The animus archetype in women is the counterpart of the anima in men. It is the image the woman inherits; so the male dwells within her. The animus projects itself onto every male she contacts with both tragic and beneficent outcome. As no woman comes across to a man in the phenomenon of her essential self because she is viewed through the anima lens, so no male in the phenomenon of his essential self comes across clearly as he is to the woman wearing the animus spectacles.

The collective unconscious, composed of the primordial dreams or forms called archetypes, must be located in the triune brain. For our purposes it matters not in which part of the human brain they are, for, as we have seen, the brain is a process, and neural messages race back and forth among the R-complex, the limbic brain, and the neocortex. But these "ground ideas," to borrow from the mythologist Joseph Campbell, are biologically grounded, millions of years old, and keep informing us out of the depths of our collective unconscious. Their projections color all of life, every relationship, each goal and every endeavor toward that goal. Precisely because they are part of the submerged iceberg, we scarcely know them; for to know them would bring them into consciousness. These powerful images are part of the stuff of which dreams are made, but also they give us nightmares. They are part of the unconscious of the person lying in the hospital bed facing death whom the pastor is trying to help. They are part of the unconscious of the man having an affair. Dreams and nightmares, hopes and fears, light and darkness, wisdom and shadow: these are of mythic dimensions. We are propelled by personal and primordial "memory traces," to enlarge upon Freud's language, that shape and color our perceptions of reality.

Then There Is Sin

Here we are not thinking of sin so much as a theological doctrine (although we cannot help but do that, as we shall see momentarily) but as profound experience. The civil war within each of us Paul knew so agonizingly and shared so honestly. "I can will what is right, but I cannot do it. For I do not do the good I want, but the evil I do not want is what I do…Wretched man that I am!" (Romans 7:18b-19, 24a). Looking for causes for this inner warfare, Paul says it is "sin which dwells within me" (Romans 7:20b). While C. H. Dodd is probably correct when he says that Paul is recounting his experience prior to his conversion, surely Paul is also painfully aware of his present divided state, which even though redeemed is still inwardly torn.[39] As Bultmann says in the context of Paul's autobiographical disclosure, "to be innerly divided, or not to be at one with one's self, is the essence of human existence under sin."[40]

This is the agony of the writer of Psalm 51:

> For I know my transgressions,
>   and my sin is ever before me.
> Against you, you alone, have I sinned,
>   and done what is evil in your sight.

As a good Israelite he would have known that this was not accurate, that it was not only against Yahweh that he had sinned, for the Israelites had almost in their genes the sense of community and how any violation of God's law infected brothers and sisters. No; the psalmist had Paul's agony in his own breast:

> Behold, I was born guilty,
>   a sinner when my mother conceived me.

Augustine could not have found the basis for his notion of original sin in the lust of the sex act creating a new foetus in Psalm 51:5. How better for the psalmist to express his sense of the depth of his sin than to say he came out of the womb, as out of a common humanity, inheriting all that sinful humanity bequeathed to its progeny? The "body of sin," a profound word of Paul's, points to no birth *ex nihilo* as far as sin is concerned.

What is this sin, then, that is at the center of our inner warfare? Now we must do a bit of theology, for sin is a theological word. Paul Ricoeur puts it straightforwardly: "The category that dominates the notion of sin is the category of 'before'

God."⁴¹ But what does "before God" mean? Biblical faith is very explicit. It does not mean the Wholly Other, the Numinous, the ultimate Mystery, although God needs to be described by such pointing words, to be sure. "Before God" refers to the speaking, confronting, giving, demanding God; that is, the God who addresses the human being. To put it in biblical language, this God is the God of the covenant. Ricoeur puts it this way: "It is…the prior establishment of the bond of the covenant that is important for the consciousness of sin; it is this that makes sin a violation of the covenant."⁴² Pedersen puts it even more tersely: "The breach of the covenant is the kernel of sin."⁴³ In covenantal understanding there is the "utterance of God and an utterance of man," a calling and a responding.⁴⁴ Within the dialogue of covenant where God speaks and the human being answers, and the human being speaks and God answers, is the crux of sin. For the human being is summoned by God, is addressed by God, is claimed by God, is told by God, "I love you and you are mine. I will be your God and you will be my person and my community. Your life will be blest if you obey my commandments." The human being is aroused, as the Edenic myth shows, but seeks to gain life on its own. The creatures cannot trust the God who addresses them and so turn to self-fulfilment. Ontological anxiety is at the bottom of human existence, and sinful anxiety is just up a step, as Kierkegaard and Tillich have so acutely shown.⁴⁵

We turn away from God, loving ourselves more than God and more than each other. Self-will, turning or curving in on the self, making the self central in our commitments and so deifying the self does not leave pride far behind. This is sin, "incomprehensible as it is, yet known to us all in the depths of our being."⁴⁶ That this warfare, this inner sickness, is known to us all as sin is not accurate. For that knowledge is not given in the social sciences, including psychology nor through natural reason, but only through revelation. It is God the covenant-maker and covenant-keeper who confronts us in judgment upon our sin, not to destroy us but to save us from ourselves. But what is in the depths of our being is the sickness that will not go away, for which we compensate in our many clever ways: sexuality, the crowd, will to power, defiance, pride, egotism, and the many forms of despair.[47] In short, we overreach ourselves, not just wanting to be "like God," but wanting to be God.[48] Reinhold Niebuhr in his Gifford Lectures has summed up the meaning of sin:

> Man [*sic*] is insecure and involved in natural contingency; he seeks to overcome his insecurity by a will-to-power which overreaches the limits of human creatureliness. Man is ignorant and involved in the limitations of a finite mind; but he pretends that he is not limited…The truth is that man is tempted by the basic insecurity of human existence to make himself doubly secure and by the insignificance of his place in the total scheme of life to prove his significance.[49]

The person to whom the pastor is trying to be of some help is a sinner (as, of course, the pastor is also). That is not a judgmental but a descriptive statement. The person has responded sinfully to the word of God, that is, to God's covenantal promises and commands, in short, to God's gracious ways toward the sinner. The person has enacted the conversation of sinful No to God's conversation of gracious Yes. But there follows a state of sin in which the self is mired. The body of humanity, of which the person is a living cell, is a sinful humanity. This humanity God joined in the person of Jesus of Nazareth to reconcile it to the divine self. Each cell in the body of this sinful humanity inherits some of the depravity of the organism from which it comes. Sin is deeply lodged in human nature, a human nature God is constantly confronting to save it from its egotistic and defiant ways. Somewhere in the triune brain is lodged the many forms of despair Kierkegaard so acutely analyzed. Profoundly, no neonate is born *de nova*, as we know genetically. Sin, no more original with ancient Homo sapiens than with us later editions, is part of what we bring with us into the world; and how well we reenact it is told in the inhumanities, the tragic injustices, we visit upon one another, in the Hiroshimas, the Buchenwalds, the South Africas, the racial ghettos in the United States, abusive homes, business addresses of greed, halls of political chicanery, to name a few. Somewhere in all of this each belongs, because the horizontal name for sin is injustice which is derived from the vertical dimension in which each answers, so often with a No, the God who wills a covenant of love embracing all humans and the entire ecosystem.

Sin is part of the profound coloring of the human scene. Each bears in his or her essential and existential being the coloration of sin. Perhaps it is through physical feelings conforming to the massive past (which we delineated in chapter1) that sin continues to reign, "exacting obedience to the body's desires."[50]

Individual Accumulation of Billions of Experiences

Carl Sagan has calculated that the human brain can process visual information at the rate of about 5,000 bits per second. But that, as he acknowledges, is much higher than other factoring such as auditory or olfactory. He has concluded that the average rate of data processing by the brain is about 100 bits per second. Over sixty years the data processing of visual and other memory recall amounts to 200 billion bits of information.[51] And, as he points out, the brain has more to do than just remember. For example, the message transactions among the two hundred million neural fibers making up our left and right cerebral hemispheres process "something like several billion bits per second."[52] The person sitting across from the pastor has a history of billions upon billions of bits of information he or she has personally experienced in his or her own lifetime, most of which is buried in the personal unconscious. Color these billions of bits of deposited information by the primordial images or archetypes of the collective unconscious. Recall the millions upon millions of years of reptilian, limbic, and neocortex data housed in each of us. Then ask: Who is this one sitting with the pastor seeking counsel or advice?

The massiveness of our pasts, long ago and as recent as a tenth of a second, is causally efficacious in every present feeling, word, gesture, thought, as we examined in chapter one. That is, the vast past is present to the instant just occurring. Let us stop time, as though that were possible, to analyze how a tenth of a second of experience occurs and includes the massive past. The man in the hospital bed anxious about his upcoming surgery is feeling a past tenth of a second of experience; that is, the present tenth of a second of experiencing is not the previous tenth of a second of experience. Let us run through just one second of the man's life, with J standing for the present tenth of a second. The present tenth is J. The previous tenth was I. J and I are not identical. J, the present tenth, is prehending or conforming to I. But the conformation is not precisely what it was with I in its tenth of a second. For God struggles with J to feel or experience I with a difference, though the difference may be so slight as not to be consciously noticeable. The moment of I is present as datum for J; J will conform to I though not duplicate I. But J is an experiencing present grappling with I and is therefore wonderfully informed and shaped by I. All this in, say, a tenth of a second.

Now remember that before J there was I experiencing or feeling H; and before that was H prehending or feeling G; and before that was G grappling with or conforming to F; and before that was F shaped in part by E; and before that was E informing D; and before that was D taking hold of C; and before that was C informed by B; and before that was B grasping A; and before that A was informed by an occasion antecedent to it. All this in one second of time in the life of the man in the hospital bed. A whole process of experiencing anxiety, perhaps, or anxiously feeling a dominant set of feelings we can denominate as anxiety. This one second of pulsating, anxious feelings would associate with millions of other anxious feelings in his life, from on-the-job competition, to report cards in school, to dates with various girlfriends, to dad's absence while away on a business trip, to quarrels between parents, to threats from peers, to imaginings about being in bed with his mother and its concomitant of castration anxiety, a sense of guilt at being wrong with God, to his actual birthing experience (the primal anxiety, the birth trauma, for Otto Rank), ad infinitum. Deepen his own personal conformal feelings of anxiety with a primal guilt embedded in the human psyche through millions of years of going against the Limit, as Sartre would put it in his non-religious language. Broaden and deepen this long and wide stream of anxiety by way of memory traces in the form of the archetype, the shadow, in the racial or collective unconscious. And lengthen the stream by the flow of millions upon millions of years as fear in the reptilian brain over turf defense, rage with accompanying fear and in the limbic brain, and ontological anxiety in the neocortex because we humans can anticipate the end to our beings: Death. The man in the hospital bed anxious about impending surgery is conforming anxiously to trillions of tenths of seconds that have become compacted in the iceberg of his unconscious, as well as to the immediate surgery and its potential threat.

All the past to which we have pointed only in a macrocosmic way in this chapter—the age-old triune brain, the collective unconscious, the sin-laced humanity defying its Creator, the billions of personal events—is out of sight to both the carer and the one to whom care is being expressed. But the massive presence of the past in the now-moment—the moment in which the experiencing client is bringing along the fantastic data from every previous moment—should remind every carer to be realistic about expectations. The past contains positive data such as occasions of hope, love, joy, fulfilment, forgiveness, transformation, even ecstacy. These are resources for constructive connections with a positive message from a caring person, messages such as a word of counsel, a timely, appropriate question, a tender grip of the hand or wrist, an unconscious facial gesture, the straightforward presence of just being there. The present moment also connects with negative occasions in the past; for example, occasions of anger, hopelessness, depression, anxiety, shame, suicidal inclinations, guilt, defensiveness. The angry, sorrowful wife of an unfaithful husband or the anxious man awaiting surgery is coping with infinitely more than what the present appears to be. Appearance can be deceptive. The skill and the art of ministry require one to be as aware as possible of the vastness of the inheritance from the past, which *is* reality and which is so easily veiled from the observer. One must not lose the awareness that what *appears* may be "an incredibly simplified edition of reality."[53]

Summary and Transition

The main point of this chapter and a main point in the entire book is the past with which the present must reckon. The past is not deterministic, but it is determining; that is, it is a vast flow of reality to which every present experiencing moment does conform in effective or powerful ways. All ministry needs to take the past into serious consideration lest it oversimplify and really miss the present. This need not lead to pessimism, but neither does it allow for superficial optimism. Hope is to be grounded in reality; that is, the past immanent in the present as the present grapples with the possibilities luring it.

But possibilities are mere abstractions apart from some Agency laboring to make them actualities or better, to give form or shape to the present moment of becoming. This agency is the working of God in our midst, as we saw in chapter 1. It is the hope for avoiding endless repetition of past into present, the hope for novelty toward attainment of new reaches of value. God is the redeeming Actor in all our processes of becoming, the divine Vision for what may be out of what was. To the working of God as the tireless Artist of beauty we turn now.

3

Divine Love as Persuasive Power

I have loved you with an everlasting love; therefore I have continued my faithfulness to you.

Jeremiah 31:3

If Charles Hartshorne, in his classic *Man's Vision of God*, has a text, it is "God is love." He sees in God's love a benevolent influence, the will to unlimited companionship. God's power is the power of influence; "perfect power is perfect influence."[1] Hartshorne has followed the lead of his mentor—and the mentor of all process thinkers, Alfred North Whitehead—who notes that Plato proclaimed that divine persuasion is the foundation of the order of the world. The "divine element in the world is to be conceived as a persuasive agency and not as a coercive agency."² Whitehead asks the question: "Can there be any doubt that the power of Christianity lies in its revelation in act, of that which Plato divined in theory?"³ But Whitehead is aggrieved that the "Galilean vision of humility flickered," overwhelmed by the model of God in the image of Caesar that became dominant in Western thought. Instead of the image of the coercive, imperial ruler, Whitehead lifts up the Galilean vision, which he characterizes in this way: "It dwells upon the tender elements in the world, which slowly and in quietness operate by love."⁴

The operation of this love is the theme of this chapter. We shall look first at God's conceptual nature, which houses the full potentiality for all attainment of value. Then we shall see how God becomes incarnate in each event with the divine lure toward new possibilities. What impact our responses make upon God and how God comes back to us with redemptive or transforming power will be our third concern.

God and the Realm of Possibility

As we saw in chapter 1, the future is the tense of possibility. It is that toward which each person must aim as that person is in the process of becoming out of the massive actuality of the past. The present does not merely repeat the past. Rather, the present conforms to the past but with some new twist, a bit of novelty, a touch of creativity, sometimes for good, sometimes for ill. This conformation to the past by way of a novel consequent is possible because the present is also facing the future where the realm of potentiality lies. So the present is a Janus-figure: looking both backward and forward in its creative instant of becoming. But the possibilities toward which the present is looking are only that: possibilities.

God's creativity makes them become real, vibrant, entreating possibilities. The omniscient God conceptualizes all possibilities as possibilities. They are different from actualities out of the past, which are also part of God's omniscience. God knows all the past as actuality and all the future as potentiality. With this total knowledge of what is knowable, God brings to bear upon each becoming moment the divine vision of what is best given the impasse of that moment. This is God's aim for the person in the throes of coming to birth between a moment ago and the best possibility God has to offer out of an infinitude of possibilities. For the best possibility is the best that is relevant to that moment of becoming. If the past moment is one of goodness, an achievement of some value, God's lure for the new moment is not simply a reenactment of that goodness, but a building upon it toward a greater goodness. If the past moment is one of evil, God's lure for the new moment is redemptive, that is, a novel consequent that embraces a value that actualizes a bit of goodness. God's vision "determines every possibility of value."[5] God, who knows intimately all of our past, knowing it without having forgotten one iota, brings to us not now and then but in every thousandth of a second, out of the divine conceptuality, that potential which is of the most value given where we are. This is God luring us, beckoning us, challenging us, with the ideal vision for that moment. Thus, God "is the mirror which discloses to every creature its own greatness."[6] God seeks to bring attainment, value, order as aesthetic harmony, peace as shalom, triumph over evil into each moment of our lives. This is God's vision for the world in no abstract sense, but in the concreteness of the passage of fraction of a second toward fraction of a second.

God Incarnate in Each Event

The persuasive agency of God requires not Plato's doctrine of imitation, but a "direct doctrine of immanence."[7] This doctrine of immanence is one of the fundamental teachings of Christianity: the doctrine of incarnation, the pristine illustration being the Christ-event. But incarnation is the constant in the midst of flux: God forever bringing the divine vision to bear in each fraction of a second. In the Christ-event we see the sharply focused activity of God, which gives us insight into what God is always about: the infusion into each moment of a tender persuasion toward meaning and beauty. Divine love is that gentle, tender working in every happening from a flower's birth, to the birth of a child, from a Mozart symphony, to a Georgia O'Keefe western painting, from the Genesis accounts of creation's mornings to Revelation's vision of a new heaven and a new earth, from God's shaping of human life in the divine image to God's reshaping of sinful human life into the fullness of the stature of Christ. As Bernard Meland has written: "God's work in history is this everlasting operation of persuasion toward meaning, beauty, and goodness."[8] Christ is the visible center of this tireless working of love to redeem humankind and all creation, which "has been groaning in labor pains until now" (Romans 8:22). The will of God is the divine operation of persuasion. Consider these words from the poet of process metaphysics, Bernard Meland:

> To speak of God's operations in history as a tender working is not to reduce it to sentiment which may or may not be ignored; it is rather to speak of it as a subtle, intricate, disciplined, restraining, resourceful, persistent, patient, and deep-working process, not unlike the skill of the artist hand, that shapes the crude clay into visible structures of beauty and intelligibility.[9]

With this vision of incarnate love in each and every event, human and nonhuman, we can see that our natures have a spiritual intent, a guided aspiration toward beauty, goodness, meaning. As we become carriers of spirit, we glorify God, whose leading is not by a beckoning finger from afar, but by a persistent presence intent on shaping our self-actualizations toward even richer attainments of value. In Paul's language, "for it is God who is at work in you, enabling you both to will and to work for his good pleasure" (Philippians 2:13). In Whitehead's words, God's "purpose in the world is quality of attainment."[10] God comes to us with the divine aim for us in the instant of our grappling with our relevant past. What that aim does is bring to us the very best possibility for us given the past we are facing. We, in turn, develop our aim in response to God's aim and the total past environment to which we must respond. Thus, God is incarnate in our struggling as we emotionally conform to the past and conceptually face a new possibility. Whitehead's summation is: "Every act leaves the world with a deeper or fainter impress of God...He confronts what is actual in it [the world] with what is possible for it." Thus Whitehead can say, "The world lives by its incarnation of God in itself."[11]

Divine love is the Word of God, to use biblical language, addressing us precisely out of the massive past of hundreds of millions of years as gathered in our triune brains, as well as out of the billions of events that our years have totaled up, including the feeling (say, of anger) of the past fraction of a second. It is God's omniscience that knows all that past as immediately present, knows all the infinitude of possibilities as conceptually present, and knows precisely which possibilities are of the highest value to me given where I am at this instant. God gently but firmly tries to persuade me with what is best for this impasse. I may not hear, listen, or be sensitive to the divine shaping. But that shaping is part of the present tense, the locus of my existentially deciding. Both faith and sin, both authenticity and inauthenticity, both adversion and aversion of value are existentially real as I decide my existence for that instant. I face the heavy hand of the past and the gentle lure of God toward the future and I decide myself, meaning I create me out of the environing past and potentially as I, in one way or another, respond to the creative, redemptive working of God, which is agape-love as persuasive power.

God the Fellow Sufferer Who Understands

The title for this section is taken directly from Whitehead.[12] Its importance lies in the fact that it underscores reciprocity between God and the whole creation, and especially between

God and each human being. Precisely because God is love, God experiences all that each creature brings to fruition out of its massive past and its relevant future. God gently presses the divine aim for each concrescing moment, as we have shown.

But that is only part of the activity of the loving God. Love is not only what God does to and for us. Divine love accepts in profound sensitivity what we do in each instant of our becoming. God feels our fruitions or temporal satisfactions, our self-actualizations, be they tragic, ugly, apathetic, beautiful, good, meaningful. Whatever we become in each instant, we become that for others, including the whole of nature, human others, God. In an awe-ful sense, we add to the experience of God. As Whitehead has written, "What is done in the world is transformed into a reality in heaven, and the reality in heaven passes back into the world."[13]

This is the meaning of one of Whitehead's famous antitheses: "It is as true to say that God creates the world as that the world creates God."[14] God participates in our creation as God gently labors to shape us toward what is best given that moment. But we create God by adding to God's everlasting being the new experience of the moment. We bring to God all shades of pain and all degrees of joy. In God's empathic love we add to the experience of God with what we make of ourselves. This is the relativity of the cosmos; it is a social cosmos; and God is the most social of all beings, because God's interpenetration with all existents is the most sensitive, the most apperceptive, the most empathic, the most amazingly connected. What we are, we are for God to experience; and that experience is a part of God forevermore.

Precisely because God feels the total emerging world at each instant, God can come back to the very next instant with the most appropriate aim, the precisely right lure for what beauty is possible, the redemptive concern in creativity's next thrust. This gives profound pathos to the concreteness of Augustine's wonderful remark: "God loves each of us as though there were but one to love." The One who knows the number of hairs of our heads, the splendor of the lilies of the fields, and the birds of the air knows each of us with an intimacy that is kept everlastingly in the heart of God, adding to the treasury that is God's omnipresent experience, and enabling God to flood each new moment with appropriate potentials to bring about a new bit of novelty, of beauty, for the ongoing creation. Charles Hartshorne has written a suggestive criticism of theological history: God "is fully sensitive both to creaturely agony and to creaturely delight. 'Sensitivity' has as good analogical right to be applied to God as 'will' or 'knowledge,' even though a much more neglected right."[15] And as Whitehead has written: "There are experiences of ideals—of ideals entertained, of ideals aimed at, of ideals achieved, of ideals defaced. This is the experience of the Deity of the universe."[16]

The strange notion that God is love but cannot suffer—a notion that is Platonic, not biblical—comes out of a faulty metaphysics where God is totally beyond the rough and tumble of existence. The doctrine of incarnation, especially as made evident in that pristine moment in history for Christians, namely, Jesus Christ, is the doctrine of God painfully and joyfully participating creatively in process. This does not introduce tragedy into the life of God, tragedy as pinpointed in the crucifixion of God's beloved Son. Human existence is tragic for God. As Hartshorne has said, "It is tragic for *any* being that loves those involved in tragedy."[17] But there is also joy, for God as the eternal Lover, prehending or feeling the world in its myriad formations, can and does move at least some of the world toward new vistas of value. As Whitehead has written, "Deity...is that factor in the universe whereby there is importance, value, and ideal beyond the actual. It is by reference of the spatial immediacies to the ideals of Deity that the sense of worth beyond ourselves arises."[18] There is joy in heaven over one sinner who repents (Luke 15:7).

God is not the Unmoved Mover, but the Mover who delights in the weaving of myriad diversities into new orders of aesthetic harmony, whether it be a crocus as the harbinger of spring, the mother and father feeding their new brood of Gallinule ducks, a teenager freed from his addiction, a dividing wall separating East and West being torn down, the breaking down of apartheid, practices dedicated to environmental salvation, or a couple rediscovering each other and forming a new ordering of their lives together. And God is moved by every new achievement of the good, the beautiful, the true. Aesthetic significance for God is the bringing into being a new actuality, out of diversity a new unity, out of what might be a moment of meaning, of goodness, of beauty. Out of possible values is woven actual value, avoiding both "the evil of chaos and the evil of monotony."[19]

Beauty is the multiplicities being directed by a cosmic Director into harmonies that enrich and enable life, but a Director who can gently persuade the discordant notes into a symphony, which is the kingdom of God always with us redemptively. So redemption is the continuing form of creation. God is the cosmic artist, the poet of the world. And God, the cosmic lover, enjoys fully and hurts profoundly, in the accomplishments and failures of the creatures the divine love seeks to persuade. Charles Hartshorne ties together beauty and love:

> The highest type of mind, the divine, contrasts with all other minds just in its infinitely superior capacity to unify the diverse. The way to find the most unity in the world is to see it as the expression of a single plan, and the only such plan conceivable is the love of God for the various forms of life and feeling, a sympathy flexible enough to appreciate simultaneously the joys and sorrows of all the multiform individuals inhabiting all the worlds. Thus the divine as love is the only theme adequate to the cosmic symphony.[20]

God's creative love transforms the world. This love is the perfect appreciation of all of God's creatures, desiring for each the utmost beauty in its self-actualization. God's love is intimate social awareness. Perhaps few have caught the profound empathy of God for all creation, and especially the human creation, as did Hosea. The prophet marries Gomer, but she proves unfaithful. She leaves to go after her false lovers. As Hosea pores over his marital tragedy, he comes to a telling insight: Is not Gomer's unfaithfulness the story of Israel's unfaithfulness toward Yahweh? And what has Yahweh always done but to keep on reclaiming Israel to redeem God's chosen ones? This reflection, which impels Hosea to bring Gomer back into their home, moves Hosea to write that amazing eleventh chapter in which he imaginatively feels after the feelings of God:

> Yet it was I who taught Ephraim to walk,
>   I took them in my arms;
>   but they did not know that I healed them.
> I led them with cords of human kindness,
>   with bands of love.
> I was to them like those who lift infants to their
>   cheeks.
> I bent down to them and fed them.

Then Hosea empathically senses God's struggle: Because of Israel's refusal of Yahweh, their God, God will send them back to Egypt, back to Assyria. But Hosea's sense is that God struggles still more:

> How can I give you up, Ephraim?
>   How can I hand you over, O Israel?
> How can I make you like Admah?
>   How can I treat you like Zeboiim?
> My heart recoils within me;
>   my compassions grows warm and tender.
>   (Hosea 11:3–8)

God enters into intimate social relationships with us, feeling in those relationships all that we feel, responding within the divine soul, and retaining the plethora of feelings in the immortality of the divine memory. Then God comes back to persuade us toward new moments that are value-laden. "All order is therefore aesthetic order, and the moral order is merely certain aspects of aesthetic order. The actual world is the outcome of the aesthetic order, and the aesthetic order is derived from the immanence of God."[21]

"God's purpose in the world is quality of attainment."[22] If that purpose is persuasively at work in our world, "too silent to be audible, too subtle to be obtrusive, too vast and extensive to be observed,"[23] what sensitivity do we need to make us aware of that working? How do we hear the word from God, not now and then in a captive moment of inspiration (although such moments are absolutely necessary), but along the entire duration of our earthly existence? In traditional theological terms, how do we become sensitive to divine grace operating so constantly in our lives to transform us into things of beauty, to make us "new or fresh creations in Christ?"

But before we analyze a new form of consciousness making us more open to the persuasive word of God, we need to look into the aesthetic mode of our existence, which is beauty in process metaphysics and shalom or peace in the biblical vision. Then in the subsequent four chapers we shall propose modes of consciousness requisite to the aesthetic mode.

4

Shalom: Gift and Actualization

Let us then pursue what makes for peace and for mutual upbuilding.

Romans 14:19

He who has shalom has everything, because it implies all the harmony and happiness which anyone can take. Therefore peace is the first and last in life.

Johannes Pedersen

*Creation is an art,
The winds would say: And God is one
Who works the artist's way.*

Bernard Meland

The human being as the inheritor of its past is, as we have seen in chapter 2, profoundly shaped by that past. The shaping is so formidable that a term like determinism might seem most appropriate to capture the heavy-handedness of the massive past. Enslavement might capture the feeling tone pervading any present inheritor if that person were to try to face the vector-powered past as it incessantly is a given for every present.

One could get extremely pessimistic about the possibility of change, even though the past comes to us with an inventory of good as well as bad. And human endeavor toward the enabling of a fellow human being to be freer, to be more fulfilled, to be released from phobias, depression, low self-esteem, pride and arrogance, and myriad other disabling or limiting experiences would surely have a damping effect on it.

But as we have seen in the previous chapter, there is a divine creativity ceaselessly at work redeeming the past in each present moment by way of a future of possibilities. That creativity is the working of grace, and perhaps the richest biblical word to express the gift of that working is *shalom,* the Hebrew word for "peace." In this chapter we examine the biblical concept of shalom and locate that concept conjunctively with the aesthetic notion of beauty in process philosophy.

Shalom: The Biblical Meaning

Shalom (the Hebrew word for peace, which informs *eirene* in the Greek) is a summing-up word, catching up in its rich conceptuality all that the creative working accomplishes in bringing together a forgiven, re-created, newly aimed soul in its individuality and in the communal nexus called covenant people to which each belongs. Jack Stotts, in his excellent study of shalom, quotes Julio Teran-Dutari on the inclusiveness of peace as shalom: "One could set forth the whole history of revelation—its substance at every stage—in terms of the biblical word which our term 'peace' attempts to render."[1] Stotts shows that the core meaning of the biblical understanding of peace is wholeness, health, security, blessing, salvation, righteousness, justice.[2] It is a rich word indeed, referring to individual peace and communal peace. In fact, the two references are intertwined, for there is no isolated individual.

Johannes Pedersen describes shalom as the "renewal of harmony," or a covenant of harmony; it is the peace prevailing in the covenanted community.[3] But it is not used in a static sense, but in the dynamic of constant renewal. Shalom is descriptive of wholeness. Whatever sullies the soul destroys integrity and wholeness. Shalom designates the full development of the soul.[4] But it is development that comes through struggle, through battling, through agony. It is the actualization of harmony, unity, wholeness in the existence of human beings who so often experience life as "solitary, poor, nasty, brutish and short," in the realism of Thomas Hobbes.[5] In the theological perspective of Reinhold Niebuhr, human beings overreach themselves to hide their finitude, and in rebellion against God want to usurp the place of God, with the moral and social consequences of injustice toward each other.[6] Shalom is no blithe pronouncement, or cheap word of solace, or even a well-intentioned assurance to bring peace of mind into a distracted, torn soul. For the soul of each knows only too well the suffering of chaos, frustration, resentment, envy—some of the motivation behind irrational, destructive, rebellious behavior as Dostoevski brought to light in his *Notes from Underground*. Perhaps this great Russian writer seems frenzied at times to many Americans still caught up in Enlightenment utopia, but as William Barrett warns us, Dostoevski "sets before us data on the human condition that it would be folly for us to ignore."[7]

Therefore, when shalom is seen as meaning reconciliation, salvation, harmony within one's soul, and the spread of that harmony or unity into all relationships, it stands for the restructuring of existence that fundamentally only the gracious working of God can achieve. It is ideally the putting on of love, the supreme grace-gift, "which binds everything together in perfect harmony" (Colossians 3:14). Shalom is the gift of God persuading the soul to refocus its aim on what the renewing life-force is bringing to it. Souls become poisoned; when the poison is taken away, peace enters. Souls go askew; when their zestful moving is redirected by the patient leading of God, peace as integrity, or wholeness, or harmony takes hold.

Souls do not exist in isolation. They are social through and through. While no soul's past is identical with any other soul's past, there is vast social inheritance. To be human is to come out of a shared past. Though appearances do demarcate, so obviously in terms of color, facial features, language, and so forth, the underlying reality that informs each and all is a social network Karl Jung captures in the collective unconscious, the archetypes, that infinitude of memory traces networking through our triune brains. The past of each is a rivulet flowing out of the vast ocean of millions of years. We are socially constituted by the past causally informing us. We belong in a common humanity, a common non-human animal ancestry, a common environmental matrix. We are organic through and through.

Shalom suggests the intimacy of interrelatedness. For example, when the underlying foundational community, the family, is whole, is in harmony, it is in peace. Towns are communities: men, women, children and sucklings, oxen, asses, sheep and goats. Peace or harmony reigns throughout the town when the people have a common responsibility, a common totality or unity, a loving regard for each and all. But the community of shalom includes the entire creation, not just human beings. Paul pictures the whole creation waiting with eager longing for redemption, shalom, for it has known futility, has been "groaning in labor pains," longing to be set free from bondage, to know the hope and fulfillment embedded in shalom (Romans 8:19–25).

But shalom is the peace of a very special community, the covenantal community, founded by God, relating God and the many creations of God, relating each atomistic bit of God's creation with every other bit, rising to climactic horizontal glory in the human community. As Pedersen interprets the meaningful covenant community, it contains a common purpose, a purpose dominated by love. In this community God's peace reigns. Yahweh is the creator of the covenant, is faithful to the covenant, reclaims the people of the covenant when they violate the covenant. Shalom is the active effect of the covenant.[8]

Jack Stotts writes: "Shalom is a particular state of social existence. It is a state of existence where the claims and needs of all that is are satisfied, where there is a relationship of communion between God and man and nature, where there is fulfillment for all creation."[9] Stotts continues in the context of covenantal existence to show that shalom is a primary term symbolizing the wholeness, health, security of a people within the covenant God has made with them. "Shalom refers to the relationships that God originally intended and that he is powerfully seeking in a fallen history."[10]

Shalom is always a relational word: signifying a quality of relationship between God and each self, between and among selves, and quite obviously within each self. In short, it characterizes the whole community of creation. The content of the shalom experience is salvation, righteousness, justice; that is, shalom is the content of grace. The creative activity of God redeems, makes new, each moment of existence so that God's *tsedeq* or righteousness/justice, God's *hesed* or mercy, God's *agape* or steadfast loyal love bring peace. Shalom is not mere peace of mind. It is reconstituted health of the organism, individual and collective, which is established and re-established. Shalom is the gift of grace. "It represents the perfect ecology of God, man, fellowman, nature. It is a comprehensive relational term."[11]

In his profound study of community and alienation, Douglas Sturm sees community as internal relations. Everything participates in everything else. His paradigm for such a concept of community is drawn from the biblical covenant, created by God, into which God calls into being new life, the life of the Hebrew people. In covenantal existence the people "were pledged to be faithful to one another, that is, to sustain one another, to care for one another, to serve one another."[12] Pedersen views covenantal existence as the result of our aims. While controversy will always be part of our mutual aims, in covenantal life we aim toward the good of the other(s). Shalom or harmony is the realization of our aims in acting together in the common endeavors. There is an organicism about covenant: souls interpenetrate, commingle, spread into one another's souls. Each leaves the traces of his or her soul in the other. When covenants are made, relationships entered into, there is no stopping the spread, the interpenetration. Mutuality is involved. "The covenant is always a psychic community, but within it everybody must give and take as much as he can."[13]

Shalom has a rich further dimension: it is ultimately an eschatological term. It points toward the future, toward possibility, toward potentiality. But it points to the ultimate One, who comes to us from beyond us. Shalom is both the gift of God and the final achievement of God. God brings shalom into the present, making possible a new now at every moment in time. What God brings to us in the way of shalom now, however, is only a fraction of its final realization. Shalom points to the ultimate fulfillment of wholeness, integrity, righteousness, justice, viz., the final reign of love in its agape form, which will be the working of the ceaseless worker in the fullness of time.

Thus, shalom is both present and future oriented: The eschatological reality of shalom is the intention of God for the whole creation, especially the covenantal human community, to bring whatever realization of wholeness and integrity is possible now in our problematic existence and to bring final, ultimate realization when the reign of God, the reign of Love, is totally enacted. Both present adumbrations and future completion are the gift of God. It is God's purpose that keeps linking the moments of time, often chaotic and demonic, into the shalom of wholeness and integrity. As Stotts puts it: "As a symbol of God's purpose, shalom provides a vision of the future for a problematic time. It orients the self and his companions toward the future, providing a structure of intentionality which affords meaning to life."[14]

John Macquarrie in his *The Concept of Peace* emphasizes the eschatological nature of shalom in creative tension with the beginning, or the original condition of the human being. The eschatological pole is the consummation or final unity or harmony at the end of history. But this presupposes that shalom has been the authentic potential for human beings from the very beginning. Macquarrie argues that peace as in shalom is both primordial and eschatological: its final realization will come, the full realization of the primordial potentiality in the human being from creation's birth. God is the giver, or the fulfiller, of the potential in the fullness of time. The Christ figure has brought near this peace in the person of Jesus. As the Ephesian church learned it: "For he is our peace; in his flesh he has made both groups into one and has broken down the dividing wall, that is, the hostility between us. He has abolished the law with its commandments and ordinances, that he might create in himself one new humanity in place of the two, thus making peace, and might reconcile both groups to God in one body through the cross, thus putting to death that hostility through it" (Ephesians 2:14–16). Some realization of this peace occurs in the continuing temporal process; full realization will be the eschatological event at the end of history.[15]

In summary, God is the source of shalom, the One who brings salvation, giving us the power to live responsibly, that is, faithfully before God. The human responsibility is to participate with God in the self's creation of itself in each instant in the passing of time. As Donald Gowan has so well summarized the biblical meaning of shalom: "Of all the words which might be used to describe what God wants most for human beings, shalom seems to be the most appropriate. As God's intention for creation, however, shalom is both a gift and a challenge to human responsibility."[16]

Beauty: A Process Perspective

I now move to locate both the gift and the challenge of shalom within the metaphysical framework of process thought.

This metaphysical vision can help us see how the gift can be actualized responsibly for the attainment of a richer quality of human existence. In making this move I am following the effort of Bernard Meland "to bring the sensitive imagination of ancient times to bear upon the disciplined metaphysical inquiry of our time."[17] Meland thus blends two sources: "the ancient myths of scripture and modern metaphysics."[18] This blending is aesthetic blending: the peace that is shalom is the aesthetic equivalent to the notion of beauty in Whitehead's vision of how every subatomic particle in existence, and especially the human soul, is constantly being lured by the cosmic Orderer into new moments of qualitative attainment.

But why this blending? Cannot the "ancient myths" stand by themselves? Do they need the framework of "modern metaphysics"? They do not need any particular metaphysical framework, though some philosophical visions are obviously more suited than others. But "ancient myths" do require to be seen and evaluated in each historical period. In each period human beings interpret their existence with the tools of that period. Tillich writes of this interpreting of existence as the "situation," by which he means those "cultural forms which express modern man's interpretation of his existence," and "totality of man's creative self-interpretation in a special period."[19] An example of such a "situation" is the very one we are in. Our world is being described as a postmodern world, a fundamental criticism of modernity, that expressed the worldview that developed out of the seventeenth century and the rise of modern science with its mechanistic view of nature, and out of the Enlightenment and its emphasis on the authority of nature and reason.

The metaphysical vision described in chapter 1 most fully expresses the concrete experience of human life and at the same time correlates well with biblical faith. It is a relational interpretation of reality in which every aspect of reality is related to every other aspect, God included. God is not the exception to metaphysical first principles, but their chief exemplification. God is that creative entity whose purpose in the world is, in Whitehead's language, "quality of attainment." Each of us is an actual occasion, or an occasioning moment, being shaped by all the givens of the past that we have acquainted ourselves with in an overview way in chapter 2. As an occasioning moment, however, we are also facing toward the future, which beckons us with possibilities relevant to our past. In between, God, who knows the massive past, that of the entire cosmos as well as the intimate total past of each of us, and who has in the divine mind the totality of possibility, including those relatively few possibilities relevant to each one in his or her existential becoming, this God confronts us with what is possible for us. God is the Orderer of reality, bringing to bear the divine vision of the best possibility in each fragment of time, the vision to which we must respond. Meland's sensitive wording of this working of God is "that there is a silent operation, a gentle working that presses upon this torrent of creativity with the dexterous hands of a creative artist. It is the work of an immensely sensitive nature within nature, brooding over the waters, giving light to its darkness."[20] And Meland continues: "It is this labor of infinite gentleness that peoples the earth, that shapes the creature of innumerable possibilities into a person of definite character and purpose. It is this silent working that blends lives together in companionship."[21] Meland's favorite characterization of this working God is the "sensitive nature within nature," and, of course, he means God within the totality of creation, every subatomic particle of all that is.

Do the honored ancient texts of scripture blend with this metaphysical vision of God's sensitive, gentle working? It is this Laborer, this Worker, this Artist gently but resolutely pressing the divine vision for each becoming, who makes possible and actualizes covenantal relations within which and out of which shalom becomes real. Since shalom is not a static, a once-and-for-all experience, but is won and lost and won again in the procession of human life, yielding, to be sure, a defining characteristic to some lives, at least, that might be characterized as shalom-laden (e.g., Abraham, Moses, Socrates, Buddha, Jesus, Francis of Assisi, Gandhi, Mother Teresa), let us examine a shalom moment, employing the concepts of process philosophy.

We locate that moment, even if only a thousandth or a millionth of a second, as the present into which a massive past flows and is confronted by a future rich with potentiality. This present moment is a Janus-moment, after the Roman god who faced both ways, past and future, guarding all entrances. The present moment looks back in conformal ways, conforming to the vast rich givens of the past, feeling the past positively, that is, embracing parts of it, and negatively, that is, denying parts of it, though it is determined by what it denies, even if less markedly, as well as by what it embraces. The present moment conditions its positive and negative prehensions of the past because of what confronts it from the future, that is, the realm of possibilities. Potentials, peculiarly relevant to this particular moment, constitute a perspective for the moment's dealing with the past. There it is, the becoming moment, about to be born out of the massive past and the potentials from the future. This is all the movement of creativity, but creativity totally open to chaos, with no rational explanation for order. Enter the divine Artist, whose gentle touch provides providence for each moment.

God is the cosmic Orderer—in Whitehead's terms, the principle of concretion. It is God, whose omniscience includes the total past in its generic massiveness and in its particular relevance for the rising or occasioning moment. It is God, whose omniscience also includes the totality of possibilities—in Whitehead's terms, the realm of eternal objects, which exist in the primordial mind of God as possibilities, fulfilling the "ontological principle" that everything exists in actual entities, and apart from actual entities there is "nothingness, bare nothingness." To our particular moment under analysis God "comes" with the divine vision of what is best for that moment as it coalesces itself out of past actuality and future possibility.

Ch 8 Linguistic Expression

"Last of" 4 modes of consciousness requisite to the aesthetic mode" (Sholom/Beauty)
(= Spirituality)

(p. 38
and ch 3)

1) importance
2) intentionality
3) imagination
4) linguistic expression

Quote on intuition — p 98 – 99 "whole duration of a person".

Section 1 p 89 – 93 nature & function of language Heidegger & child [?]

Section 2 p 93 bottom – 98 mid – language in the church – preaching, in relig life, faith pp 96 pic of God "after the manner of Christ"

2 pm 13th – Thes.

Whitehead calls this activity of God the "lure" of God, among other terms, meaning that God wills or purposes a definite outcome for this moment in the process of becoming. It is God who brings to bear upon the occasioning moment the vision of a particular outcome, an instance of novelty emerging out of the physical prehensions of the past and the conceptual prehensions of the future.

This guiding, luring, purposing of God I would equate with the biblical notion of the word of God. It is not a word spoken now and then, which is not the biblical notion of *dabhar/logos* either, although there are sublime, ecstatic, pristine, ultimate moments, as Christians affirm in Jesus of Nazareth. The word of God is "the creative Activity which is divine," to borrow from Norman Pittenger.[22] To every occasioning moment the word of God comes to lure that moment into the quality of attainment possible for that moment. God does not determine the outcome of the moment, but provides for it a vision of what it might become. This is the aim of God for each particularity. God presides over the birth of each moment in the profound sense that God's word, or aim, or vision for that moment is part of what each occasion experiences, though rarely are we conscious of that aiming.

God's word, or aim, or vision is God's love for the world. Of that love Whitehead has written, "It is the particular providence for particular occasions."[23] God is creatively at work in the microcosmic bits and pieces of each of our moments. Meland has poetically described this working: "Creativity is attended by the gentle art of a patient hand, pressing this ruthless chaotic flood into events with meaning and beauty...The power of gentle might! This is the power of the spirit that is in God, and at work in each of us and in the world."[24] This is the word of God communicating the divine self and its vision for each moment to every happening taking place in the universe, and especially to every human moment of occasioning. God intends beauty, the attainment of a harmony of disparate parts into a unity. The human organism, reacting to its total environment of past and possibility, is led by the creative worker of values to create a new moment of order, of wholeness, of oneness. Thus, the new moment is added to the procession of previous moments, a moment of discord and tragedy, or a moment of wholeness or beauty. God aims for beauty, leading every instant of becoming by his vision of truth, beauty, and goodness.

This constitutes the occasioning moment, a moment of severe responsibility. For what does it do with God's loving aim for that moment? How does it respond to the word of God to it? How does it yield itself to the gentle pressing of the divine hand? There will be attained unity. But that unity may be discord. This is still the aesthetic experience. Diverse feelings are unified. But this may be the unity where evil abounds; or it may be unity aiming at a higher perfection that includes discord. It may be unity at a mere animal level, appropriate to a pig but not to a human being. It may be unity at the stage of mere repetition, where habit dulls the sensitivities. Or it may be unity striving toward some higher end, and failing, but the failing may be a novel move forward. As Whitehead has written, "an actual fact is a fact of aesthetic experience."[25] Peace as shalom is not limited to achieved goodness, which might be a totally boring achievement. Peace as shalom is the actual occasion of experience aiming toward God's aim for it. There is teleology in shalom: God's aim and the occasion's aim for a creative unity out of the vast multiplicities that are givens for that moment of experiencing.

In process metaphysics there is a strong emphasis on the function of choosing or selecting "ends," of aiming, of value formation. God reaches into the becoming of a human subject to give to that subject the divine word (biblical) or the initial aim (process): what God's best vision is for that tenth or thousandth of a second of creativity. The subject responds to the givens of the massive past that are present to it, to the possibilities that lie before it, to the particular "lure" or "will" of God in that coalescing or "deciding" moment in the passage of time. Thus, the initial aim of God and the subjective aim of the aborning self come together, for richer or for poorer. Here, in this very nexus, the biblical understanding of sin, the Whiteheadian understanding of evil, the whole sense of tragedy, "what might have been," are located. And, here, too, growth as into the "fullness of the stature of Christ," is achieved. This is the location for shalom in the biblical sense—for beauty, in Whitehead's terms. But this shalom or beauty is not without the possibility, and often the realization, of discord. Biblical shalom, or Whitehead's understanding of peace, is not mere peace of mind or psychological calm. More often than not there is striving toward unrealized ends or goals, and this may be far richer than mere attained unity.

Shalom cast in the process mode of becoming is never a static realization. Such realization would fulfill Whitehead's understanding of evil. Shalom is in process, the self-selected bent of the soul in its attempting to meet faithfully and responsibly the aim or purpose of God for it along the duration of its temporal negotiating between past actuality and future possibility.

There is in Whitehead a strong emphasis on the function of choosing or selecting of "ends," "goals," possibilities relevant to each moment. God wills, purposes, gently brings the divine vision to bear. But how do I, a macrocosmic self, containing billions of events of microcosmic proportions (e.g., subatomic cellular structures composing body and brain) "hear" the word addressed to me, "see" the vision God sees for me, "feel" the gentle hand guiding me, "sense" the sensitive nature artistically working on me, so that *my* aim meets God's aim for me to bring into creation a shalom experience of beauty and peace? In essence, how does God get my attention? That is the question we look at in the next four chapters, which is in part at least the question of how ministry functions in the mode of shalom.

5

Importance

Importance is derived from the immanence of infinitude in the finite.
Alfred North Whitehead

Your whole life now must be one of longing...And this longing must be in the depths of your will, put there by God, with your consent.
The Cloud of Unknowing

Importance. The word is not common to theological writings nor even to philosophical writings. One might wonder why a philosopher of the stature of Whitehead would begin his *Modes of Thought* with the elucidation of the notion of importance. But when we reflect on what is important in our daily lives, we certainly come to see that importance is a primary mode of every minute of consciousness. It is small wonder that Whitehead characterizes it as an ultimate notion.

Our daily lives are crowded with multiplicity. There are time schedules, job responsibilities, home responsibilities, friend and family relationships, school involvements, decisions about leisure, handling of stressful situations, balancing the needs of the self, of others, of the environment. This vast multiplicity demands choosing, selecting, deciding. What we regard as important informs us in our selecting process. In deciding we depend on importance, that is, what is important to us, what interests us, what we value, what grabs and holds our attention. Second by second (actually, nanosecond by nanosecond), we are putting together our lives. Most often, of course, the dilemma of selecting, or choosing, or deciding is scarcely noticeable. Routine is in charge. We would be utterly frenzied if it were not for those daily rituals by which we go about much of our daily routine. If not the unconscious, at least the preconscious takes over. But the hours are still full of decision making: how to deal with temptations in the marketplace, at the office, in the home, at school, at play; what to do with the drives of aggression, sexuality, power; how to handle our anxiety, hostility, guilt; how to cope with our need for affection, self-esteem without underdoing it or overdoing it, self-actualization without jeopardizing community; how to do some kind of balancing of the several institutions making demands on us: family, church, volunteer organizations; how to negotiate between private need-fulfilment and others' need-fulfilment. All of these more dramatic decisions are part of what goes on relentlessly as the self is constantly in the process of forming itself. In deciding at each turn of events we depend in large part upon what is important to us, what interests us, what we hold to be valuable both for the moment and down the way. At some level of consciousness we pay attention to what we regard as important. Of course, there are degrees of importance, but whatever is important to us furnishes us vision, myopic or long distance, for the moment at hand and the goal or goals into the future. Our attention is sustained by some sense of importance.

That sense of importance depends on perspective. Perspectives help to tell us what is important. Perspectives are culture laden, conveyed in the stories that trace the life of our universe, the rise of philosophical visions, the rational or theological explanations of our religious institutions, the moral, social, economic, and political values by which a people live. There are many perspectives speaking to our pluralistic human creaturehood. And each of us makes his or her own some part or parts of the many perspectives that inform us. These are what we value, what we regard as important, and what we employ as guides along the way of putting our lives together. These perspectives are multidimensional, ranging from ultimate to penultimate, from the eternal, that is, God, to the very temporal. The myriad contexts of our lives dictate our interests, our purposes, our temperament, our directions, our responses, our zest, our apathy. Our ideas of what is important are born of these many contexts and the perspectives they engender. This sounds like Jamesian pragmatism where the value of an idea, an outcome, an action, a decision is its "cash value." While I am not now dealing with any theory of truth, it is helpful to borrow from James at this point when he says, "The practical value of true ideas is…primarily derived from the practical importance of their objects to us."[1]

Peter Bruegel's painting "Christ carrying the Cross" (1564), is a powerful illustration of importance guided by perspective. A great crowd in hastening to an execution on a hill on the horizon. It is a crowd in a holiday mood. In the center of the crowd Christ is collapsing under the weight of the cross he is carrying. The only mourners are a small group buried in tears of grief. The figures in the foreground in the crowd are engaged in multiple interests: arguing, romancing, doing business, fighting, gawking, playing, hastening or plodding to the scene of execution, some on horseback, some walking, a few running. Most people in the painting who are on their way to the crucifixion do not even see the Christ. Nor are they looking. They are preoccupied with what is immediately important to them, with matters certainly not unimportant in themselves, but matters that do not allow even elbow room for the suffering One in their midst whose very execution they have come to witness. As Gustav Gluck commented on the true-to-life painting: "It is the topsy-turvy world which does not even trouble itself about its Lord."[2] Being "busy here and there" (1 Kings 20:40), we, like the crowd in Bruegel's striking pictorial comment, sometimes lose perspective on what is crucially important here and now.

Importance does derive from the values we place on the many objects swirling around and informing our lives, whether those objects be money, prestige, pleasure, security or mere subsistence, support communities, or drive fulfilments as in sexuality, egocentricism, aggression, or power. What we value creates the perspectives by which we judge what is important. In today's world economic values are often set over against environmental values: the logging industry versus the spotted owl; clean air versus costly regulations with impact on the ozone; rampant individualism versus communal and covenantal respect, issuing in justice as fairness.[3] Many of our perspectives by which we determine what is important emerge out of the day-by-day struggle to exist, to live, to live better. These perspectives are constantly with us, dominating our thinking, planning, scheming, acting. Right here may be the essence of our current problems. A theological vision, an eternal perspective, an ultimate value seems not to be informing us on what is really important. Perspective born of an ultimate dimension does not minimize other perspectives. Indeed, it enriches them, but it enriches them in ways that change our notion of what is important.

In chapter 1, I described a process metaphysical framework. In that framework process theology furnishes us an ultimate perspective, the source of unity out of multiplicity. Whitehead focuses on this source of unity:

> We start from the notion of two aspects of the Universe. It includes a factor of unity, involving in its essence the connexity of things, unity of purpose, and unity of enjoyment [read, actualization or realization]. The whole notion of importance is referent to this ultimate unity. There is also equally fundamental in the Universe, a factor of multiplicity.[4]

We have described the "factor of multiplicity," the common experience of each of us struggling with diverse contexts, diverse values, diverse claims, struggling to become a unity out of the vast multiplicity, a one out of many. But there is an ultimate unity, a primordial ordering not by coercive heavy-handedness but by persuasive love, to bring out of second-by-second struggling the very best unity possible for that impasse. God is incarnate in each moment of becoming throughout the universe, gently trying to shape the self emerging out of its somewhat unique past by giving to it the very best possibility or set of possibilities that self might actualize. Thus, God is concerned with the attainment of value, the realization of importance, throughout the entire process of becoming. God is not lost in multiplicity. God is creatively, redemptively active in bringing the divine vision of what is important to bear in the soul of each in the vortex of multiplicity. As David Griffin has put it so succinctly: "A cosmic Source of Importance exists." And he suggests how this Source of Importance operates:

> God does not create unilaterally, but inspires the creatures to create themselves by instilling new feelings of importance in them...The all-inclusive story is what the Divine One is doing with the world: creating beauty...At our level, the beauty of our lives, which includes intellectual fineness and moral and religious beauty (the

"beauty of holiness") as well as appreciation for and creation of beauty in the more usual sense of the term.⁵

God tells us what is important, or tries to, as God communicates to us in each moment the divine vision of what is best for that moment and for the effects of that moment on the self, on the rest of the community of creation, and on God, as we shall see below. God has a vision for each instant of becoming, a vision as to what is finest for that moment in its immediate impasse. So Whitehead writes, "Importance is derived from the immanence of infinitude in the finite."⁶ Thus, importance is an ultimate notion, tied into the ultimate aim of the universe toward the attainment of value in a single occasion or moment in the becoming of a self, in a species, in a society. I wonder if this is something of what the psalmist may have been intuiting as that poet said to Yahweh, "You hold my lot…I bless the Lord who gives me counsel; in the night also my heart instructs me" (Psalm 16: 5b,7). Could it be that in the night God has a better chance with us than in the day so overwhelmed with multiplicity?

And there is a second way in which the sovereign Good provides importance to our lives. Not only does God bring to bear upon us the divine vision for each moment; God also receives into the divine nature whatever we put together in each moment. Each moment is a new event in the world's life, passed on to the self's next moment, to all the self touches, and passed into the very life of God. What we do, what we are, God experiences. And those experiences are part of God's experience forevermore, part of God's omniscience. So importance includes what we deposit with God, adding to the experience of God second by second. God inherits from us: our good, our evil, our superficialities, our moments of importance. Thus the immediate event has some eternal value. Our imprint is not upon the life of the world alone, but upon God as well, who carries in the divine experience the effects of joy and sorrow, of qualitative attaintment and tragedy, as they transpire on earth. Whitehead's closing sentence in *Process and Reality* underscores the significance of this notion of importance in these words: "The insistent craving, that zest for existence be refreshed [is justified] by the ever-present, unfading importance of our immediate actions, which perish and yet live for evermore."[7]

God bears in on every single moment of our lives with the divine vision of what is best in that particular impasse. What we decide—that is, what we do with our prehensions or feelings of the past and our responses to new relevant possibilities God brings to us—is received within God. God *experiences* our "decision," our actualization, what we finally create within this milieu. God is affected by what we "decide." We add to the eternal experiencing of God the novelty of what we have just created, adding joy, pain, sorrow, tears, pleasure to the very life of God.

Importance? Every moment is freighted with it! What can ministry do to help us deal more self-consciously with this ultimate notion? I can only suggest a couple of ways at this point, coming back to that question in each of the topics in this section of the book.

Whatever the theological position of the one ministering, one tenet that is crucial to the notion of importance is providence. Whitehead focuses the "love of God for the world" in this trenchant sentence, which was quoted in the last chapter: "It is the particular providence for particular occasions."[8] While Whitehead and John Calvin interpret very differently the words "particular providence," Calvin uses those words to pinpoint God's "sustaining, nourishing, and providing for every thing which he has made."[9] Calvin flatly rejects any notion that God is Creator "only for a moment, [having] entirely finished all his work at once." Rather, Calvin urges that "the presence of the Divine power may appear to us no less in the perpetual state of the world than in its first origin."[10] Calvin's concern in "particular providence" is similar to Whitehead's: a constant providing presence actively engaged in the ongoing life process. While they interpret *how* God goes about the divine work of providing differently, the emphasis on providence is crucial.

Whatever the form of ministry—preaching, teaching, sharing, training, caring, spiritually forming, administering—the ministering person needs to help us all to become appreciatively aware of the indwelling, creating God who is at work in every instant of our becoming. *Every moment becomes important because every moment is a transforming moment.* The Eternal One is luring that moment into a creative unity. God's vision for that moment is here and now: whether it be a lovemaking moment, an on-the-job moment, a moment with friends, a moment of study, ad infinitum. Thus, the vertical and the horizontal meet. Many of these moments are ritualistic, formations of habit, and habit is significant, for life cannot always be lived on tiptoe, nor should it be. But habit dulls the soul. If we can be taught that there is a "particular providence" for each occasioning instant along the duration of time; that God works in and through all the structures of existence, shaping meaning and character; that there is a "sensitive nature within nature" to borrow from Bernard Meland, struggling with the patience and dexterity of a creative artist to bring about renewed and transformed people, we can become more aware of what is important. Then the ultimate, God, brings value to the penultimate: to our work, families, play, churchgoing, friendships. This is the grace of God at work. Meland has put almost poetically this working for each "particular providence":

> "The power of gentle might! This is the power of the spirit that is in God, and at work in each of us and in the world." [11]

Ministry must help us to envisage, and labor with, this source of importance. For *how* we respond to the gentle working of God is felt by God and becomes part of God's experience forevermore. Thus, importance has an eternal significance. It derives from God and goes back to God. In essence, ministry is the prophet's role of pointing us beyond our immediacies that so saturate us to the One speaking in those very immediacies the creative, transforming word of new life in the very midst of the old. Thus, we become spiritual, not in any escapist sense, but in the down-to-earth sense of our spirits, being molded out of clay by the gentle, creative, loving Artist whose joy is to make us more and more resemble the One in whose image we were intended. So incarnation continues as God is present to us to fashion us in the image of the Christ who is our finest clue as to what God looks like. Ministry must lift up this working of God, this providential caring in every particularity of our lives, so that we do not lose perspective by getting so immersed in the sensationalist appeals of television, for example, in the stressful conditions of current living, in the penultimately important matters of economics, family, school, even church, that we violate what gives real significance to importance.

Prayer plays many roles in our continuing lifelong odyssey, but a major role is to keep before us what is important. There is an amazing unanimity among the classical writers about prayer. Saint Francis understood it as a time of storing up grace and power through union with God. There is Pascal's famous line, "The heart has its reasons, which reason does not know," where Pascal located prayer as the heart's loving of God.[12] Howard Thurman understood prayer as the movement of the heart toward God.[13] Thomas Merton expresses what prayer is: "Prayer…means yearning for the simple presence of God, for a personal understanding of his word, for knowledge of his will and for capacity to hear and obey him."[14] Rufus Jones said prayer "is born of our need for spiritual fellowship…where there often is a palpitating sense of divine presence." Then he concluded: "The very substance and essence of prayer is 'mutual correspondence.'"[15] Prayer is the heart of the human being, the heart of religion. It is not opposed to reason, nor is it largely petitionary. Using William Temple's profound insight, prayer is intercourse with God. It includes petitions, but much, much more. It is not a sporadic cry out of an occasional need; nor is it getting something from God. Prayer as spiritual intercourse, or intimate communion with God, is a habitual attitude, not simply an occasional act, although it is an act of experiencing that is deepened by set times of prayer. As Fosdick put it, "The practice of prayer is necessary to make God not merely an idea held in the mind but a Presence recognized in the life."[16]

Prayer seen as the heart of religion helps to clarify our dominant aims, what we are really after, what we crave, what is our basic demand on life. As Fosdick went on to say, what we desire is really our prayer: We pray the prayer of dominant desire. Speeches addressed to God may not be prayers at all, or spurious prayers at best. "Prayer is dominant desire, calling God into alliance."[17] So as we examine our prayers we find our life perspectives, what really matters at the heart of things. Thus, we can come to know what is really important to us.

Ministry needs to help us clarify what prayer is and help us to examine our prayers to know what we really desire. In our study of how faith is formed, a study of how 210 people came to faith, prayer was the second most important factor, next to caring people.[18] But what we heard most of the 150 laypeople involved in the study saying as they discussed prayer was: "We really do not know how to pray." As they shared their faith stories, many seemed to be echoing the disciples of Jesus, "Lord, teach us to pray." There was very little criticism of their pastors, either past or present, on the part of the laity, but they did feel somewhat strongly that they had not been taught what prayer is nor how to pray, and many suggested that prayers from the pulpit were not helpful models to enable them to overcome a deeply felt deficiency. How deep that deficiency is can be gleaned from William James's conclusion that prayer is the core of religion.[19] It is instructive to quote James at this point: "Prayer in this wide sense is the very soul and essence of religion...Religion is nothing if it be not the vital act by which the entire mind seeks to save itself by clinging to the principle from which it draws its life. This act is prayer...[is] the very movement itself of the soul, putting itself in a personal relation of contact with the mysterious power of which it feels the presence."[20] James concludes that without prayer religion is only a philosophy.

Importance depends on perspective. A major way to perspective is prayer, not in vain exercise of words nor in "mere repetition of certain sacred formulae,"[21] but in the intercourse between the soul and God. All ministry requires of itself this deep religious experience, out of which its own wounds can become healers in the service of God. This fulfills the vision Henri Nouwen lifted up in his *Wounded Healer:*

> The man of prayer is a leader precisely because through his articulation of God's work within himself he can lead others out of confusion to clarification; through his compassion he can guide them out of the closed circuits of their in-groups to the wide world of humanity; and through his critical contemplation he can convert their convulsive destructiveness into creative work for the new world to come.[22]

6

Intentionality

When you search for me, you will find me; if you seek me with your heart.

Jeremiah 29:13

While we long and seek for God, God is longing and searching for us.

Gerald May

These words are coincidentally written on New Year's Day: the day of resolutions. And what are resolutions but some of our intentions for the year just beginning? These intentions are what we want, wish for, maybe even long for; what we are aiming to accomplish, maybe even to change our behavior (to stop smoking?). Our intentions are future-oriented, tied in with goals. They are the will in action consciously desiring something. They tend toward new meanings, new understandings, thus involving some rationality. They are in touch with some of our feelings, as we feel disgust with past actions, disappointment with ourselves, the wanting to revivify feelings of excitement or accomplishment by extending ourselves into the future. In short, our intentions are future oriented, directed toward some object such as an idea or ideal, and carry at some level, often a most superficial level, our commitment.

But these intentions, so common and so conscious to us, are underlaid by intentionality, our capacity to have intentions. In his excellent chapter "Intentionality," Rollo May concludes, "Intentionality is an assertive response of the person to the structure of his world. Intentionality gives the basis which makes purpose and voluntarism possible."[1] And May continues: "Intention is a psychological state; I can set myself voluntarily to do this or that. Intentionality is what underlies both conscious and unconscious intentions. It refers to a state of being and involves, to a greater or lesser degree, the totality of the person's orientation to the world at that time."[2] Now we are far deeper than any New Year's resolution; any intention to do or make a change; any willful desire to re-cathect our energies toward the world after suffering a grievous loss of one to whom we had deeply cathected ourselves, to borrow from Freud; any wish projected onto another, whether a human other or God.

Intentionality is of the structure of being: fundamental to our intending, our aiming, our entire future orientation. Thus, intentionality is a primary factor in causality. A person constructs himself or herself by what one makes of that self through choices that are future facing, through what one intends, the intention or the aiming toward a goal in the future being a response to the appetitive structure of each being. Gordon Allport argues that "the most comprehensive units in personality are broad intentional dispositions, future-pointed."[3] We live out of the past toward the future in the present. Crucial to this striving, or growing together of the self, are our intentions, which in Allport's understanding are our *characteristic* interests, those that characterize us each moment in our interlocking struggle to become.⁴ In a profound way each must ask: What am I trying to bring about? For we are our responsible, final cause (not in Aristotle's sense of "final cause," of course). And my causing of myself, my bringing myself each moment into being, comes out of the past that pushes me and a future that pulls me. It is on that future that I focus. My intention is to bring about a certain outcome. Therefore, the direction of our striving is the unifying theme in our lives.⁵ In a moment we shall focus on the source of this intentionality that May and Allport have found so essential to each personal life. But before that we turn for a rich clue to Martin Heidegger.

Heidegger pinpointed his existential/phenomenological philosophy of Being in *Dasein*, identifying Being with each concrete, existing human being. Dasein is each human self in its "being there." Its existential structure is not deduced by a theory of humankind but analyzed phenomenologically, that is, by letting the concrete self tell or say what it is. At the center of Dasein, each existing self, is an ontological structure that Heidegger names "care" (*Sorge* in the German). At the center or core of each human being is care. Each person engages in, spends itself, devotes itself in and to the world he or she has concern about. Each human projects itself toward what it cares about. Our will, wish, addiction, and urges are founded on, and emerge from, care. Our anxiety, common to all of us, grows out of our care, that is, out of our very structure, which propels us toward the objects of our care. Heidegger put it pithily: "Dasein's Being reveals itself as care."⁶ Thus, Dasein, that is, each concrete self, is "Being-ahead-of-itself," exercising its ontological character by standing in the present aiming toward the future in response to its essence, care. Care leads to concern; we have concern(s) toward which we project. Care is our essential nature.⁷

If I understand Heidegger correctly, his understanding of the ontological structure of a human being as care underscores, or more correctly, locates intentionality. The essence of being a human being is tending toward, or taking care of, or being concerned about or with. We are "stretching" toward something. That's what an intention is. To intend something is to have a purpose, a goal, a design about it, whether it be others, ourselves, our pets, our God, our job, our natural world. Intention involves attention: We tend to pay attention to what we care about or are concerned about. Heidegger's brilliant analysis of Dasein as essentially care helps us to locate intentionality at the very center of the self. It is out of the very structure of our being, described as intentionality or care, that "I can set myself voluntarily to do this or that. Intentionality [or care] is what underlies both conscious and unconscious intentions. It refers to a state of being and involves, to a greater or lesser degree, the totality of the person's orientation to the world at that time."[8] Answering our intentionality, we move toward objects, or away from objects, or against objects. Our lives are tendential. At our center there is the immensity of human longing, the longing that persists, the profound care that is forever stretching toward fulfillment, the Intentionality that is always seeking. As the psychiatrist Gerald May has concluded: "It is only religion—if religion only will—that can speak to the immensity of such longing and the depth of its ramifications. Each religion does speak to this, in its own sometimes forgotten ways."[9]

This brings us, then, to the Judeo-Christian way of speaking to this ontological longing. Biblically there is a structure of intentionality, and that structure is the human soul. The Hebrew word is *nephesh*, which has as its essence intentionality as direction, purpose, aim. The nephesh is zestful, questing for adventure, reaching out beyond itself. The nature of the soul is to aim with the far view as well as the near view in perspective. As Pedersen in his classic, *Israel, Its Life and Culture*, has described nephesh: "Nephesh hungers and thirsts; is greedy; is satisfied; feels joy, sorrow, love, hatred, hope, despair, etc."[10] The soul is absorbed in its orientation "towards something to which it is led or towards which it directs itself."[11] Thus, the soul is lifted up to God (Psalm 25:1); waits for the Lord in whose word it hopes (Psalm 62:1,5; Psalm 130:5); becomes centered in God and controlled by God. Spirit (*ruah*) is the controlling notion, whether one's own spirit or an outside spirit, and it is most often an outside spirit, say of Baal or Yahweh, that is controlling. In Israel's finer moments, it was the ruah of Yahweh controlling nephesh; but in its sinful, disobedient, times it was the spirit of harlotry or unfaithfulness that possessed the Israelite nephesh.

The human soul is an organism whose predominate capacity is appetitive and volitional.[12] It is always adventuring, and happy is the soul when its questing is fulfilled by the ruah or Spirit of God. The prophet's major condemnation was against the whoring, idolatrous, unfaithful, disloyal soul. The wise soul seeks the Lord, and when its appetitive, desiring nature is sated, the soul is complete, happy, restored.

Souls are social through and through. They act on each other; they interpenetrate each other. In their mutual interchange they receive from each other strength, sadness, joy, and so forth. When souls are united they gain a common will. Totalities are created. Thus, Israel is a covenanted and covenanting community with a common character running through the souls within it. A soul is partly an entirety with itself and partly an entirety with others. Pedersen says, "That which is received into the soul must influence the character of the whole, just as, in its turn, it takes its character from the given stamp of totality."[13]

Finally, the soul is responsible for the ideas it contains, and those ideas direct the soul "towards something which it can receive into itself, and by which it can be determined."[14] "Therefore, it is of the greatest importance which ideas fill the soul."[15] The king going to war must fill his soul with victory before the fight. If he does not win, it is because he did not go to war as a soul of victory. Action is part of the idea within the soul. It is critical what the soul strives for—its appetitive nature—since that determines what it is filled with, which in turn determines its totality, its peace (shalom), its satisfaction.¹⁶ So shalom, as peace and harmony, belongs to the soul hungering and thirsting after God. Finding its home in the Lord, the soul suffuses and directs the body (Hebrew, *basar*), that is, the outward person and the heart (Hebrew, *lev*), the inward person, thus forming the wholistic organism. This is spiritual existence, as the soul, captured by God, directs the entire organism toward the aims or lures God has for it in each moment of its becoming. Spiritual existence is thus living beyond itself by way of living totally from the initiative of God.¹⁷

Now we are at the point where we can bring nephesh as we have described it into the process model for understanding ourselves and our world. The value in this is to locate as precisely as possible where human intentionality and divine action correlate.

In chapter 1 we described the process metaphysical framework within which we are working as each self arises out of a massive past and stretches forward toward an infinity of possibilities within the milieu of which it must actualize itself. God reaches to the self to offer it the divine vision for its becoming in that instant, a new moment in the world, a moment laden with value because of God's dream for it then and there. In biblical language God speaks the divine word to each instant of becoming, that word being God's luring the occasioning moment to what God envisages is the best for what it might become. The occasion itself has its deeply laden intentionality, its ontological care, its nephesh straining or stretching toward a future not yet. God meets that soul, the Spirit or ruah of God confronting it with God's best vision for it, relevant to where it is and where it has come from. Whitehead terms this offering from God the initial aim, the gentle luring of the creative Orderer who envisages all actuality and all potentiality and gives vision to what is best in each moment of becoming. Each soul, straining, seeking, the organism of appetition, having prehended or grasped its actual past and confronted by God's initial aim toward it, in that instant has its own subjective aim: what it intends. So the soul, stretching toward fulfillment, may have many objects attracting its aim. God's aim is in the midst of frightful competition. The soul's aiming is the expression of what interests the occasioning moment, what it desires, what "grabs" it. Hopefully, God's aim, God's vision, God's word will meet the nephesh in redemptive, creative power, not the power of coercion but the power of persuasion, the power that fixed Moses at the burning bush. God got his attention; novelty was born; Israel had a powerful new leader. God struggles with every aborning creative moment, to bring a new aesthetic order into being, and "the aesthetic order is derived from the immanence of God."[18] To expand on this I quote more fully from Whitehead:

> The order of the world, the depth of reality of the world in its whole, the value of the world in its whole and in its parts, the beauty of the world, the zest of life, the peace of life, and the mastery of evil, are all bound together—not accidentally, but by reason of this truth: that the universe exhibits a creativity with infinite freedom, and a realm of forms with infinite possibilities; but that this creativity and these forms are together impotent to achieve actuality apart from the completed ideal harmony, which is God.[19]

Is not this aesthetic order, this shalom, this identification of the human soul with the divine Spirit, wrought by the immanence of God, seen in Isaiah's call in the year that King Uzziah died; in Jeremiah's keen sense of being chosen and appointed; in Hosea's amazing insight in the midst of his marital tragedy, the insight into God's redemptive way with faithless Israel that impelled him to bring Gomer back; in Job's answer to suffering; in Amos' creative discovery of the nature of justice; and at the pinnacle of immanence, in Jesus' faithful servanthood so incarnational of

God that his relationship to God has to be expressed in terms of Son of God?

It is precisely where nephesh reaching out, stretching toward, intending, tending, caring, is met by God's Spirit addressing nephesh, gently trying to lure, direct, give vision to, that spirituality has its home. This is not a once-and-for-all confrontation. It is a durational confrontation, as along the passage of event upon event, the passage to which clock time and calendar time do not do justice, God is constantly bringing the divine vision, appropriate to each actualizing experience, to create a shalom moment and order. Spirituality envisaged in this way is not Platonic spirituality of soul over against body, the immortal soul imprisoned in a mortal body. Paul, for example, does not set body and soul in opposition to each other. Paul's dualism is flesh versus spirit, that is, flesh is the person out of Christ, spirit the person in Christ. Flesh denotes the human being under the domination of sin, spirit the human being indwelt by Christ.[20]

Spirituality within this process framework in which shalom is our major key includes all bodily needs and desires, vocational or job needs and aims, social interpenetrations and inclusions at all levels, communal responsibilities, and ethical sensibilities and relationships with the total natural environment as the locus of the first covenant God made with the divine handiwork. If intentionality as intention, care, concern, wish, desire, aim is of the human essence, spirituality is our mode of responding to the divine to work continually to create something of beauty. The spiritual intent of our natures is hungering and thirsting after righteousness, which is far more than good, ethical deeds, as important as they are, though they can so readily be captive to mere moralisms. Our spiritual intent must be that the Spirit of God will create in us and develop in us an "appreciative consciousness" that builds an aesthetic order in each self and in the community in which each and every self lives.

To be redeemed, to be made new creations in Christ, means that "through commitment to that tender working which is the

Creative Source of all being, all goodness and beauty, all discrimination of truth and rightness...can be made sovereign in our lives...The lure of Christ in this drama of redemption has always been that of the visible center of man's dedication."[21] That dedication is organismic as we are inherently related to the totality of creation, to every microcosmic as well as macrocosmic event. It is ultimately the dedication of agape-love, the very love which is the nature of God, the essence of divine grace bestowed upon us, and which must constitute the direction of our intentions toward ourselves and every other self and entity. This could be very daunting if it were not that God, our Unlimited Companion, to borrow from Charles Hartshorne, is constantly directing us in unfailing love toward the creation of beauty, and forgiving us and healing us when we fail our spiritual intent.

In his superb chapter on saintliness, a word describing the spirituality to which I am trying to point, William James reminds us of what religion at its best is: "the genuinely strenuous life...an inner state which before all things is one of love and humility, of infinite confidence in God, and of severity for one's self, accompanied with tenderness for others."[22] Our souls searching, seeking, finding, are made for the rendezvous with God that religion is all about. True, they go awhoring, prove unfaithful, pursue false lovers, as the prophets remind us. But our souls are made to live with God, to live from God, to live toward all others. This is the major meaning in the creation story that we are next of kin to God, created in the very image of God. We are tarnished images, but God refuses to leave us tarnished. There is a "characteristic affection to which our nature is liable,"[23] to borrow a phenomenological conclusion of James. No wonder we are restless until we rest in God.

It is the clergy's high calling, though certainly not limited to them, to help each soul to direct its searching. Whitehead made an utterly amazing statement in the early 1930s: "My thesis is that a new Reformation is in full progress. It is a re-formation; but whether its issue be fortunate or unfortunate depends largely on the actions of comparatively few men, and notably upon the leaders of the Protestant clergy."²⁴ He thought the "divine persuasion" was gently trying to bring about a new world order through such religiously motivated leaders as Gandhi and the Viceroy of India (Lord Irwin). Whitehead expected a few religiously sensitive leaders to alert the religious sensibility in the world to work with the divine persuasion that could work within the brute forces in the world to bring about a new measure of harmony: directing purposes and modifying behavior. Is this a set of conformal feelings in Whitehead reaching back to his Anglican childhood home? Was Whitehead paying a filial debt to a beloved clergy father? Whatever indebtedness he felt, Whitehead was never a sentimentalist. He knew the agony of tragedy (what might have been), the massive heaviness of the actualized past, the blindness of so much human aiming. He knew what the Western world had done to Christianity: "Caesar conquered; and the received text of Western theology was edited by his lawyers…The brief Galilean vision of humility flickered throughout the ages, uncertainly."²⁵ The clergy were responsible. Yet he saw the clergy as requisite to a re-formation. Did we clergy fail the divine vision, and in that failing do we share some responsibility for the twentieth century, becoming one of the most infamous, murderous, slaughtering times in human history?

If human intentionality must be directed by the gentle persuasive immanence of God, then clergy especially called and trained to work with the divine Artist and to help faithful others to let their aims be directed by persuasive Love must be held responsible for a re-formation to take place. Now in our postmodern world clergy have another kairotic "moment" to help the religiously faithful to learn how to meet the caring God as that sensitive Being struggles persuasively to change the world. The modern world that began with the fifteenth century and its Renaissance vision and matured after the Enlightenment of the eighteenth century is now coming to an end.²⁶ The modern world has seen individualism run rampant, to the tragic loss of community. The individual is a social self organismically related to the totality of human social selves, but in our modern epoch community has become alienated.[27] The patriarchal model coupled with white supremacy has established a hierarchical effect, patriarchy preceding by centuries the modern era, of course, to further the loss of community. Our anthropocentricism has both lost sight of the intimate relation between human beings and the natural order and abused the order of nature to the dangerous degree of possible environmental tragedy. While science, both in its theory and practice, has been a major positive force in the modern world, as in health advances, space explorations, communications, and technologies in agrarian and other productive endeavors, it has also contributed to mechanization of our lives, questionable emphases on consumerism, and the threat of nuclear disaster, both militaristic and environmental.

If we are in a postmodern world, trying to deal with some of the problems arising out of the last few centuries, is it not rather naive to look to the clergy to give us much help to build a new world? The answer to that question depends upon how seriously we take God's initiative for creative change and whether God calls some people not for special place and privilege but as servants to help others respond to God's creative vision. Does God have a vision for every actualizing self at each instant of its becoming? Does each self have a fundamental intentionality, a deep care or concern toward something to which God aims or focuses the divine vision? In this existential moment, can the human nephesh and the divine ruah, soul and Spirit, meet and in this meeting form a moment of beauty or shalom, to bequeath its formation to the next moment of becoming? To borrow from Meland, our spiritual capacity is furthered as we become more deeply awakened by the God struggling to bring new richness to all our relations, beginning with God and including all human relations, and the environment upon which we are so dependent.[28]

We need to be creatively guided into this new awareness, guided by the scriptures, the church, the life, teachings, death, and resurrection of Jesus Christ, so that the goal of the church as H. Richard Niebuhr envisaged it, "the increase among men of the love of God and neighbor,"²⁹ can be increasingly realized. And as Niebuhr continues, love of God and neighbor "is the demand inscribed into infinitely aspiring human nature by the Creator; its perversion in idolatry, hostility and self-centeredness is the heart of man's tragedy; its reconstruction, redirection and empowerment is redemption from evil...The purpose of the gospel is not simply that we should believe in the love of God; it is that we should love him and neighbor."³⁰ The aspiration intentional in us, met by the luring of God's loving aim, gives us the spiritual sensibility to struggle to fulfill Paul's ultimate challenge at the close of his hymn to love: "Pursue love" (1 Corinthians 14:1a).

The clergy are called to serve God, our fellow creatures, and the natural environment, that the love with which God loves us might become the dominant desire of all hearts, and the fundamental action of all lives. Ministers, through their preaching, teaching, pastoral care, and administrative duties need to have this as their highest vision: helping themselves and all others within their ministry to become open to the incarnate and incarnating God who longs to shape us into vessels of love. This is ministry enabling the larger ministry of the whole church. The minister is called to help create people of beauty, the shalom every heart yearns for, that the total people of God, the church, might become in their own turn ministers of beauty. Ministry is essentially the Socratic midwife helping each to be reborn into the kingdom of God, the kingdom of agape-love, where each is "oned with God," fulfilling the "naked intent," of the soul.³¹

The minister's vocation, employing the redemptive resources furnished her or him and the opportunities in worship, in teaching, in pastoral care, should have as its ultimate goal helping each soul in travail—as we all are—to know where to look and what ultimately to look for. Perhaps Carl Rogers has provided a very appropriate model: to give real meaning one "should put his hand over his mouth and *point*."[32] In a profound sense the minister, among a plenitude of others, of course, is simply the one whose soul has been touched by the God of grace and who has been called in sundry ways to point to the One who cares about each soul as though there were but one to love, and whose own intention is to draw that soul into a beatific vision of life lived with God and every creature the divine hands have shaped, and are constantly reshaping. Employing the traditional means of grace, the minister is called to help each person to know where to look, how to aim, so that that person's intentional structure, an ontological longing for the Ultimate One, can be met by the ever-seeking God. This would seem to be the heart of the ministerial calling: to help prepare all the people of God to be ministers creating in their relatively small neighborhoods of life something of beauty. And so, longing intentions of each soul might be captured by the divine Intention to increase love of God and neighbor in our world.

7

Imagination

Every real conversion is first a revolution of the level of our directive images. By changing our imagination, we alter our existence.

Paul Ricoeur

Mary Warnock, in her excellent study of imagination, says that imagination is a "power of the human mind...which enables us to see the world, whether present or absent as significant, and also to present this vision to others, for them to share or reject...Its impetus comes from the emotions as well as from the reason, from the heart as much as from the head."[1] Warnock has underscored in these words two major functions of ministry: to form models or pictures of God, God's workings, God's claims upon us, and to communicate these models, images, pictures to others for their re-imagining. For it is fundamentally our images, our pictures, our models, our metaphors that become the media theology uses to talk about God and by the way of such discourse to confront us all with the Holy, the ultimate Mystery, the awe-ful Wonder for which we use the term God. As Ian Ramsey has so well summarized this image-making, model-constructing operation of the mind: It enables us "to talk about God, about the Christian claims for the significance of Jesus of Nazareth, about certain distinctive patterns of behavior and certain future hopes rather than take refuge in a holy silence."[2]

We are well aware of the images, models, pictures, metaphors that are abundant in the Bible and in the church's theological history which have been the rich functioning of the imagination, one of the primary modes of human consciousness. God has been pictured biblically in so many rich images: father, king, judge, shepherd, creator, unfailing lover, Lord, sun and shield, friend, refuge, deliverer, redeemer, rock, among many other imaginative pictures. And throughout the history of the church God's people have added yet other images: for example, His Majesty (a favorite picture of Saint Teresa of Avila); Sally McFague's models of God as mother, lover, and friend of the world, which world she imagines as God's body; Bernard Meland's picturing God as creative Artist; Whitehead's image of God as the "great companion—the fellow-sufferer who understands"; and Simone Weil's image of God as bread for which we are eternally hungry.

Our images, pictures, metaphors are formed by our imaginations to carry us from one place to another, which is the root meaning of metaphor in the Greek. They transfer us from one thing, or one word, to another, as the word father pictures for us what a heavenly Father might look like, or a mothering figure might suggest an infinitely nurturing deity, or the sheep herder might picture an eternal Shepherd. To be sure, this is analogical image-making, with all its attendant dangers. But imagination must work out of experience, as we shall see. Amos

Wilder in his *Theopoetica* puts the problem in these terms: "Imagination is a necessary component of all profound knowing and celebration, all remembering, realizing, and anticipating; all faith, hope, and love! When imagination fails doctrines become ossified, witness and proclamation wooden, doxologies and litanies empty, consolations hollow, and ethics legalistic."³

In our secular world our problem—maybe the major one—is how to recover a sense of the sacred. Wilder urges that we need to "repossess the mystery of the Cross and its glory in a way that would speak to all."⁴ Imagination is the crucial mode to do this to get beyond the "normal" and the "reasonable." To bring out the richness of this structure from consciousness we shall examine the mode of imagination with the religious and theological imagination in the forefront of our concern.

Imagination is the ability to construct images of things. David Bryant, in his superb study *Faith and the Play of Imagination*, underscores the power of synthesis, as does Warnock, meaning by synthesis "bringing together the similar in the midst of the dissimilar."⁵ Image-formation is a basic aspect of cognition. We create images out of our experiences of individual objects, which we form into a general image. Imagination is a functional power allowing us to form concepts out of our limited human experience. This formation is not limited to conscious activity, for as we have already seen in chapter 1, we are shaped by the massive past that informs our imagination. It is our total actualized past, mostly unconscious, whether Jung's collective unconscious or Freud's personal unconscious, that informs our imagination. The informed imagination has the power of re-presentation, re-presenting objects in new and different modes, as when the image of the human father re-presents an ultimate or divine Father. Thus the imagination is symbol-producing, the symbol operating analogically.⁶

The past has shaping power, providing us with symbols by which we perceive and organize our lives. These symbols provide us with meanings, which help us to shape our thinking and acting. Our imaginations synthesize and put things together in the present out of the massive and rich past toward the future. As we saw in the last chapter, intentionality looks to the future, and it does so by the imagination, which refines and resynthesizes images from the past, creating visions of what can be. In an example David Bryant used, when the "Hebrew prophets envisaged the coming rule of God, they spoke of it in terms of a new and better Davidic ruler, a transformed Mosaic covenant, a New Jerusalem, an exodus far surpassing the first exodus."[7]

We think about God imaginatively; that is, we form images out of our experience, no image, of course, defining the very being of God. But the images carry over from sensory experience, for example, a mother figure enabling us to create a vision of what a nurturing God is like. We know what a rock is; so when we sing the hymn "Rock of Ages, cleft for me, let me hide myself in Thee," we are confessing our weakness and our need for divine protection. When we think about, or talk about, God as steadfast or unfailing Lover, while we do not know in human experience this quality of love, we do know love in some forms, such as sexuality, friendship, human loyalties, and we therefore have a basis for image-building as we yearn for a love that is never failing. Much of our language is metaphorical. As we have already seen, the root meaning of metaphor is to carry us from one place to another, to bear us along, say, from a common experience of eating bread at a common meal to eating the bread of life around the liturgical table. The metaphor of bread gives the power to Jesus' discourse about the bread that is perishable and the bread that lasts, "the bread of life," in John 6. As Bryant keenly observes, "a metaphor cannot be an occasion for logical coercion, but only an invitation to look for oneself."[8]

Metaphors are not logical arguments intending to be rationally conclusive. They open our eyes and ears to ways of looking at and hearing about the world and guide us toward new understandings of our life within God's orbit. But the word *understanding* must not be limited to rationality. Metaphors, and all images, speak to, direct, excite our affective and volitional natures as well. We human beings in that marvelous creation story in Genesis are told that we are created in the image of God; then we are told by the serpent to eat the forbidden fruit, for then we will be like God himself. Here is a wonderful play of images in which we are to see ourselves: next of kin to God and exploiting that kinship in defiance of God. No series of logical statements could possibly say what these images have said, for they force us to open our eyes to what we are in God's image and what we have done to deface that image. Nietzsche's famous conclusion is not far in the distance: "If there were a God, who could bear not to be God. Therefore, there is not God."

Russell Kirk, who has written about T. S. Eliot's "Christian Imagination," can be helpful to us. As Kirk points out, Eliot's "religious imagination opened the eyes and comforted the souls of many who had been seeking for images of truth."⁹ Eliot exercised his synthesizing or reproductive imagination, the human mind's power to bring into a fullness the rich experience of time past, time future, time present, by putting into the artistry of poetic words, if ever so subtly, the claims of Christianity, pouring new wine into old wineskins, as in the "Four Quartets," in which his religious imagery held sway. And he exercised the productive, creative imagination that, as Kirk points out, combines "former experiences into new images," what Whitehead calls the novelty of the present moment created out of past actuality and future possibility. Finally, Eliot employed the moral imagination, by which Kirk means "the power of descrying people, despite their weaknesses and proclivity to sin, as moral beings meant for eternity, in brief, the dignity of man."¹⁰

"The Love Story of J. Alfred Prufrock" has these marvelous moral one-liners:

> Do I dare
> Disturb the universe?...
> I have measured out my life with coffee spoons;

And then the continued existential anguish:

> Should I, after tea and cakes and ices,
> Have the strength to force the moment to its crisis?
> But though I have wept and fasted, wept and prayed,
> Though I have seen my head (grown slightly bald)
>   brought in upon a platter,
> I am no prophet—and here's no great matter;
> I have seen the moment of my greatness flicker,
> And I have seen the eternal Footman hold my coat,
>   and snicker,
> And in short, I was afraid.[11]

And choruses from "The Rock" are prophetic in the sense of speaking forth from life's depths the religious question:

> CHORUS: What does the world say, does the whole world stray
>   in high-powered cars on a by-pass way?
> VOICE OF THE UNEMPLOYED [*more faintly*]:
>   *In this land*
>   *No man has hired us...*
> CHORUS: Waste and void. Waste and void.
>   And darkness on the face of the deep.
>   Has the Church failed mankind,
>   or has mankind failed the Church?
>   When the Church is no longer regarded, not even opposed,
>   and men have forgotten
>   All gods except Usury, Lust and Power.[12]

It is clear, as Kirk observes, that Eliot held that "imagination is the eye of the soul."[13]

This lengthy illustration from T. S. Eliot should not be construed as a model for clergy. Kirk has said it correctly:

The reason why Eliot's poetry moves us to think deeply on the claims of Christianity, and why the typical pulpit sermon today does not so move us, is that Eliot possessed imagination in the highest degree, dreaming the high dream; and the average preacher, no matter now good, is not so endowed with imagination.¹⁴

The use of Eliot is strictly to enforce the importance of images, pictures, metaphors to convey the power of imagination, and to remind us clergy that it is images and metaphors that help us to "see as," that is, in Warnock's analysis, to construct pictures out of past experience, religious and nonreligious, to enable us to construct and reconstruct the essence of the gospel in the light of each concrescent moment. Immanuel Kant used the German word *Einbildungskraft*, the power of making or building images, pictures, or representations of things to identify this mode of our human consciousness. Enriching that mode is a basic function of ministry in creating a thing of beauty. For a major work of ministry is to help each of us achieve a more sensitive structure that is essential to work with God, whose "purpose is quality of attainment," in the words of Bernard Meland.¹⁵ Meland strongly urges the development of our human capacity for sensitiveness, for getting beyond our preoccupations, as with television, our mere survival concerns, our idolatry in and of the marketplace, our racist, sexual, ethnic prejudices and biases, in order to make possible the spiritual life, which lives toward ultimate concern. By "ultimate concern" Meland means "religious awareness in which God, whose working is creativity, becomes known and consciously accepted as sovereign in man's life."¹⁶ The function of images, pictures, representations is to enable imaginative consciousness to become alive to the silent working of God, the redemptive Being seeking to fulfill our destiny. Meland urges that our faith hangs upon our readiness to provide the structures of consciousness, including imagination, as part of our higher dedication.¹⁷

If there is a hunger for transcendence and for ecstasy, imagination must feed the hunger; imagination not born of poverty, but of plenitude; not a superficial groping or spiritualizing, but a profound reaching out of the tradition that has formed us toward the beckoning hand of God reaching for us to grasp us, which is the essence of faith: to be grasped by God. Our intentionality is at work craving a new vision that seizes us and liberates us from our alienations, our arrogance, our greed, our individualism of "me first," our isolation from the natural creation we are arrogantly misusing, our failure toward those not like us from whom we are isolated. That new vision is in part the gift of imagination.

The picture I have in mind is Jesus' sermon, the Beatitudes: "Blessed are…" Mere rational explanation, important as it is, will not fire us to aim toward the realization of gentleness, mercy, purity of heart, peacemaking, and the other characteristics of the kingdom Jesus spelled out. Grace alone has the power to invigorate us toward the kingdom goals. But imagination plays a crucial role in the working of grace, for it helps us to see where we have come from, whither we are going, and what we are doing out of our past toward our future—imagination that is captured by the word of God, especially as that word has become enfleshed in that amazing, steadfast, solitary life that is the hero in the sense of his obedience.

We as believers participate in the ongoing operation of the divine in which we encounter our evil and our disobedience, and find our forgiveness, the grace of God's redeeming love. But our participation is not normally enlivened by creedal statements used as affirmations of faith or responses to the preached word. Our participation is made alive as models, images, metaphors, representations grasp our attention and quicken us to respond in faith, hope, love. For example, the classic, "We Shall Overcome" has been a powerful motivator in the struggle for racial equality, as has been the message of Martin Luther King, "I Have a Dream," with its personal and rich imagery. The hymns

"Let There Be Peace on Earth and Let It Begin With Me" and "I Want to Be More Like Jesus," rich in concrete imagery capture the intentionality toward community that lies deeply within each of us.

In our age of individualism, bereft of community, we desperately need a new, imaginative exploration of covenant and its implications for life together, within the human community, nature, and the subhuman species of animal life. The rediscovery of the individual-in-community is possible through the imaginative reading of the Bible in its rich Judeo-Christian sweep when the mind of the believer is captured by the deep persuasions of the Spirit.

The "reading of the Bible" is part of private devotional time, but is also inclusive of the "right preaching and hearing of the Word," in Calvin's teaching, and teaching of the Bible in the educational functioning of the church. Since people live by their images and dreams, and since childhood is such a vital time for image and dream formation, teachers of children need to be very aware of the lively imaginations in the class around them, and help feed those imaginations with the biblical images and metaphors so that imagination in later years can synthesize and reproduce those images and metaphors into creative productions for the living of their lives.

This will help God to make alive day by day, hour by hour, the spirituality that makes possible the courage to be, not in merely a rational sense or even an ethical determination, but in the Tillichian sense of the "courage…that is rooted in the God who appears when God has disappeared in the anxiety of doubt."[18] Tillich means, of course, the courage of absolute faith when one is "grasped by the God beyond God," that is, the Ultimate One beyond all our human definitions.[19] Perhaps some pastors should be teaching the children and not just adult classes on Sunday mornings, helping to build into these young imaginative minds biblical images that they can synthesize into appropriate models, images, metaphors in their adult journeying where overwhelming experience of the sacred is so existentially needed.

What I have in mind is the suggestion made by Rainer Maria Rilke in one of his many letters, that our images are our future waiting to be born. So many of us—perhaps all of us—have such limited, self-serving, defense-laden images, repeated ad nauseam, that the future is almost bound to be stillborn. We suffer a terrible imprisonment within our images, resulting in our compulsion to repeat. New images, models, metaphors are required to synthesize or reproduce the past into productive or creative novelty. For example, in our present late-twentieth-century culture, the image of a king produced by a history of demonic kingships is hardly available to image God in a respectful, awesome, adoring mode. Perhaps we can never reclaim that image as Israel saw it in David and the Bible appropriately applied it to Yahweh. And perhaps the image of Father in our time of tragic neglect and other abuse by so many fathers must at least be balanced and corrected by the model of God as Mother (*agape,* creating); God as Lover (*eros,* saving, healing); God as Friend (*philia,* sustaining, companionship) as proposed by Sallie McFague,[20] realizing, of course, that all images or models, including biblical ones, are limited by our finitude and imperfect, sinful natures and therefore require updating and correcting as we are able under the guidance of the Holy Spirit. Nevertheless, model-making must go on to allow the imagination to play in the sense that Gadamer uses the model of playing as cited by David Bryant.

In play the players lose themselves in the play. "Genuine play absorbs the players into the structure of its movement and hence shapes their consciousness in its movement...Moreover the essence of the game is located in the movement of the game rather than in some substitute underlying the game...Play is found nowhere but in the play itself."[21] This play is the back-and-forth movement within the game that is the primary role of imagination as play: a dialogue between the power of discovery and the power to disclose, allowing "the new to appear through novel syntheses," the dialogue playing itself out among persons and between persons and the world.²² Imaginative preaching and teaching take images shaped by the Judeo-Christian tradition and images shaped by our daily experience to give rise to and guide both theological reflection and action. Thus, fundamental spirituality is enabled by the play of imagination to let the eyes see, the ears hear, the soul feed on the divine Reality, the consummate Artist, gently trying to help us to see what Job saw.

The appearance of God to Job is borne in several images, including laying the earth's foundations, stretching a measuring line over it, supporting the pillars on which the earth rests, giving birth to the sea as it floods from the womb, calling up the dawn and assigning the morning its place, and so forth (Job 38—41). Job, who acknowledged that he had previously known God only "by the ear of hearing" when confronted by the awesome Presence of the Lord confessed: "But now I see you with my own eyes" (Job 42:5). When Job "saw" God, was caught up by that awesome experience, he took the courageous stand born of that revelatory experience: "Therefore I despise myself and repent in dust and ashes." (Job 42:6). God's presence forced Job into himself, causing him to see himself and to yield out of his depths from which his life had taken form and to examine that life in the mode of confession. So he was enabled to grasp life in some new way. Although overwhelmed by the confronting majesty, Job was guided by an "infinitely tender hand" and enabled to "await with deep humility and patience the birth hour of a new clarity," to borrow Rilke's fine words to a budding poet.²³

This waiting in humility and patience was the way Simone Weil described her deep spiritual journeying. Her favorite image was "eating," and she was ever "looking," "waiting," and "walking toward" to feed on the transcendent One who is the bread of life.²⁴ Weil's formative spirituality was deeply embedded in her identification with the homeless, the hungry, those caught in the tragic life in France and England during World War I. It was out of those experiences that "eating" became such a vivid image for her faith expression, along with the "looking" and "waiting," by which she meant waiting in patience for that food that would satisfy her needy soul.

Deep religious experience and expression, whether of Job or Weil or their innumerable fellow travelers, are the fulfillment of the questing nephesh in its divinely ordained intentionality for the bread of the spiritual life. Directing the nephesh are the images of our creative imaginations, seized by the ruah or Spirit of God, whose gentle hand tries to shape the emerging life toward what it may yet become. This is the human soul, whose aiming is not mired down in merely survival or entertainment interests, but is directed toward possibilities of fulfillment in the forms of love, justice, humility, patience, gentleness, companionship, "and the kind of profound awareness relating to man's ultimate destiny which may give rise to wonder, reverence, and devotion toward what is of ultimate concern."[25] For this destiny to become possible from the human perspective, we must provide and excite those structures within human consciousness that can entertain the creative Spirit hovering over all creation and yearning to incorporate the human species into the patterns of beauty the divine envisages. Imagination is a key part of the human being's sharing with the creative Artist in creating things of beauty. Then the psalmist's dream may become more a dream realized:

> Steadfast love and faithfulness will meet; righteousness and peace will kiss each other (Psalm 85:10)

What is this embrace but the embrace of shalom, the shaping of our lives into the beauty God profoundly wants for us all? Ministry must seek to do for us all what C. S. Lewis said George MacDonald did for him: "baptized his imagination." Whether it is preaching, celebrating the sacraments, teaching, or pastoral care, a major mode of consciousness, imagination, needs to be immersed in the biblical and theological images and metaphors as well as in the secular models, which bear our actualized past, and be guided into a productive present by God's lure rich with new possibilities. The psalmist caught this luring of God in this imaginative line, "Your Word is a lamp to my feet, and a light to my path" (Psalm 119:105), a line metaphorically inspiring. Then perhaps we can produce the fine fruits grown in the "genuinely strenuous life," which is what William James meant by religion.[26]

8

Linguistic Expression

I suggest that the development of systematic theology should be accompanied by a critical understanding of the relation of linguistic expression to our deepest and most persistent intuitions.

Alfred North Whitehead

The twentieth century has experienced major studies in the nature or essence of language. While it would not be appropriate in this chapter to deal with all of them, two will inform us as we look at ministry in its linguistic expression. First we turn briefly to Heidegger and then to Whitehead.

For Martin Heidegger language as speech is a fundamental mode of being: *Dasein.* For each concrete human being, the Being-in-the-world *(Dasein,* the "being there"), speech is existentially involved, that is, rooted in the very "constitution of

Dasein."[1] It is speech that gives understanding to Dasein and interprets that understanding. "If it is true that man finds the proper abode of his existence in language—whether he is aware of it or not—then an experience we undergo with language will touch the innermost nexus of our existence."[2] Being expresses itself in language and so attains an experience in doing so.[3] In one way or another language transforms us into itself as it expresses itself. Perhaps this is most notable in poetry, which prompted Heidegger's analysis of Hölderlin's great poetry, and it is very evident in the psalms and other poetic-like scriptural passages such as Paul's hymn to love in 1 Corinthians 13—14:1a. Language, for Heidegger, constitutes for us an experience along the way, transforming us into itself.[4] Thus, language is an event through which human beings unveil themselves, an existential or experiential event that is responsive to the initiative of being, Dasein, one human being to another.

Raising this language-event into theological terms, which Heidegger never does, the human Dasein, the concrete existential human being, unveils himself or herself in faith-language, responding to the Word of God that comes through Jesus Christ, the Word made flesh, the written word or scripture, and the preached or shared words of faithful people of the word. The most appropriate linguistic event in response to the ultimate word may well be prayer.[5] What an event prayer is in creating Dasein, each existential human being! What depth this gives to Harry Emerson Fosdick's description of prayer as "spiritual intercourse with God."

James Robinson extends Heidegger's concept of language to the event of faith in these summary words: "Existence is itself essentially linguistic, and faith takes place within our language, which is our answer—not just a secondary *expression* of our answer to God." Language is much more than just our vocabulary. It is the "encompassing medium for understanding and conveying meaning in which we exist."[6] Being expresses itself in language, even the divine Being, as well as, of course, through other signs, i.e., nature, as Yahweh did to Abraham, Moses, and the prophets, and especially in the theology of Christianity, through Jesus Christ and his disciples. God speaks in Genesis and the worlds come into being. The Word which was God — God in the mode of eternal communication to the creation — became flesh and dwelt among us. That enfleshed Word revealed what God wanted all to hear. And the church through the ages has been involved in the linguistic event of proclaiming salvation, the unfailing love of God.

Now let us turn from Heidegger's powerful analysis of language to Whitehead's equally powerful analysis of how language creates us. In his *Modes of Thought* Whitehead pinpoints the primacy of language in these powerful "one-liners":

> Speech is as old as human nature itself. It is one of the primary factors constituting human nature.[7]

> Speech is human nature itself...[8]

> The mentality of mankind and the language of mankind created each other.[9]

> The souls of men [*sic*] are the gift from language to mankind.[10]

> The account of the sixth day should be written, He gave them speech, and they became souls.[11]

In this celebrating of language by picking up its essential nature as being creative of us humans, on what does Whitehead base this predication? He had in mind the present actualizing moment out of its past, which is efficient causation, and toward the future, which is final causation, as we have seen in chapters 1 and 2. The past, which includes Jung's collective unconscious and Freud's personal unconscious as well as the totality of fractions of seconds of events in every life, is the given for every present moment as the self brings together or coalesces its vast data from all the past moments into a new instant of becoming.

This past is where our memories come from, but it is a past consciously remembered in only a fraction of its totality. It is the past of all the previous moments of deciding, whether the human being be a year old or eighty years old. The sweep of this actualized past is not only in small ways available to us in every now; it informs us massively in every now.

The self deciding in every fraction of a second is also confronted by the immediate and longer stretch of the future where the possibilities lure us toward a new moment of novelty. It is God, in whose omniscience this infinity of possibilities have their home, who brings to each of us in our present deciding moment the best relevant possibility for us now. God's omniscience, of course, also includes the totality of the past, for without this divine memory relevance for the present would not be possible. So God brings the divine lure to bear upon us, beckoning us in that fraction of time we call the present "toward meaning, beauty, and goodness."[12] This is God's tender working in each now, creating and recreating out of the past and toward the future a new creation, a moment of novelty. As Meland poetically phrased the creative working of God:

> When it was morning,
> God took the good earth
> And held it to His lips,
> And breathed upon it:
> Breathed silently upon the dry earth.[13]

Every event in the present instant between its completed past and its potential future is a repetition of this age-old happening, as Meland envisioned. This is a form of fulfilment of Revelation 21:5: "See, I am making all things new." Language has a special function within this entire process of becoming. Language, both spoken and written, helps the present actualizing occasion to tie in with the past duration of actualized occasions by provoking memories, and to aim toward a relatively new moment in response to the tender creative beckoning of God. Whitehead wrote, "Life is the enjoyment of emotion, derived from the past and aimed at the future."¹⁴ Language becomes a prompter of such emotion, one of its enlighteners, helping to galvanize every emotion derived from the past and aiming toward the future. Language, both written and spoken, conveys the need for referencing to the past in the present toward the future. Language, whether read from a book, viz., the Bible, sung from a hymn book, preached from a sermonic text, taught in a classroom, or shared where two or three are gathered together, elicits memories, some long buried and others nearer the surface, and reengages one in the processive moment of remembering toward the future where intentionality is directing. Whitehead once said, "It is one function of great literature to evoke a vivid feeling of what lies beyond words."¹⁵ Cannot the same be said of the spoken word? For all language, written and spoken, can evoke feeling tones out of the past into the immediacy of the moment to which the person responds in his or her own creative synthesis of past and possibility.

I am not arguing for the total adequacy of language. But I am arguing, as did Whitehead, that there is a fundamental connectedness of things, the many in the one and the new one issuing forth to add to the many. And language, both spoken and written, helps the present actualizing occasion to tie in with the past duration of actual occasions and to aim toward a relatively new next moment, which is the production of novelty between memory and the new possibility. As Whitehead stated this point: "Each occasion of experience has its own individual pattern. Each occasion lifts some components into primacy and retreats others into a background enriching the total enjoyment."¹⁶ Language is one major force for this enrichment.

The particularity of linguistic sounds, say from the pulpit, elicits reactions or responses to the past with its myriad events or occasions being drawn into some degree of consciousness or immediate awareness, which we term remembering. New questions may be formed in the congregant's mind, old questions or feelings revisited, new determinations made, feelings of guilt brought to the surface. The immediate preaching/hearing moment—in Calvin's words, when the word is rightly preached and heard—is an abstraction unless it can engage with the route of actual occasions called the past and with the new possibilities luring it that are the initial aim of God for the immediate moment.

This referencing of the words heard by the auditor who must relate them to the past and reenact them by way of imagination toward the future may, for example, bring into play the commandments to love God and the neighbor as oneself. But that creative work of imagination presupposes antecedents in the memory system and a genuine attempt to be open to the communicating God. Language is in the present tense evoking past linguistic memories and intending toward the sensitive working of God to create a moment of beauty in the present. This moment of beauty was framed together by Whitehead in the Galilean vision: "It dwells upon the tender elements in the world, which slowly and in quietness operates by love; and it finds purpose in the present immediacy of a kingdom not of this world…[But] the kingdom of heaven is with us today…God is the great companion—the fellow-sufferer who understands."[17] I wonder how much of this Whitehead derived from the words of his clergy father and how his own poetic words grew out of those memories from home in England.

Heidegger and Whitehead, among many others in this century, have shown us the intrinsic value of language in creating us even as we create language to express our concrete being, Dasein, our actualizing of ourselves in each moment of our becoming. Yet we cannot lay hold of the numinous, the holy, the sacred with words, for mystery rebukes our speech. How appropriate the prayer of Shankara, whom Huston Smith calls the Saint Thomas Aquinas of Hinduism, which begins with this invocation: "Oh Thou, before whom all words recoil."[18] Still, as Smith avers, "words and concepts cannot be avoided. Being the only equipment at our mind's disposal, any conscious progress toward God must be made with their aid."¹⁹ Words become pointers, hopefully pointers in the right direction, pointers to the One who is the wholly other, the numinous, the holy, to use some of Rudolf Otto's language, but the One who addresses us. Words like those of Otto, of biblical witnesses, of theologians and preachers through the centuries are linguistic expressions to enter into faith's dialogue with God and within the covenanted community in response to the speaking, addressing God.

We must be careful not to limit linguistic expression to preaching and liturgical services, although those are the contexts most of us might have in mind when discussing language in the context of the church and ministry. But ministry is much larger than the professional ministry, to which I shall return. Ministry is the servant-role of the people of faith, that is, the Christian faith. The people of faith form with God the covenanted community, the people with whom God has covenanted to be their God and they God's people and to share their faith—calling as servants of the Most High. Part of that sharing is the vision Jesus had of his ministry—which he took from Isaiah 61:1–2 and preached in his first sermon back home in Nazareth:

> The Spirit of the Lord is upon me, because he has anointed me to bring good news to the poor. He has sent me to proclaim release to the captives and recovery of sight to the blind, to let the oppressed go free, to proclaim the year of the Lord's favor. (Luke 4:18,19)

The basis for the servant work of the people of God is hearing the word of God, responding to the word of God, and inviting others into that relationship which is promised through the word. Language is the primary human shaper of our faith and its work. David Bryant has made this point: "Faith arises when one is captured by the disclosive power of faith's language."[20] God is not just an idea, merely a theological form. God is the One in whom we trust in the existential mode of trust, as Kierkegaard argued so forcefully. This trust is the fulfilling of nephesh, or soul, as it strains toward answering the Spirit of God luring it moment by moment into ever new actualizations of love, thus fulfilling the servant mode of Jesus that is the goal of the church, as Niebuhr has taught us.[21] For Christians the life of Christ "is the supreme moment in religious history," as Whitehead has observed.[22] That "supreme moment" throws light on every other moment, for it pictures God active in every moment after the manner of Christ, in whom God revealed the divine self. Because of that revealing of God we can know that there is a tender patience leading the world, a sensitive humility kneeling beside the world, a deep caring willing for the world wholeness and joy. That patience, that humility, that caring are disclosed in Jesus' servanthood. His ministry gives us our best clue into the constant activity of God and what God requires of us in our ministry.

The ministerial acts of the people of God are expressions of our servanthood, but they depend on linguistic expression to disclose Christ's vision and exemplification of servanthood as the chief clue to what God is saying to us in our time. In every time language is the interplay between the divine and the human. All through scripture the role of language is disclosure. God speaks to Abraham, an old man of seventy-five, to leave home and go to a far country, making a covenant with him to establish the nation of Israel. God speaks to Moses, deepening and enlarging the covenant. God speaks to and through the prophets, enlarging the vision of the covenant and the responsibilities of trust and action for the people of the covenant. And in the fullness of time "the Word became flesh and lived among us...full of grace and truth" (John 1:14).

The Old and New Testaments are fundamentally a conversation, or better, a series of conversations, between God and the creation, especially the human community. God is the speaking, disclosing God. The people of God are the hearers who also speak, for covenant is the community of dialogue, the people answering God and talking to each other. Martin Buber's great I-Thou concept is sharply put in this statement: "All real living is meeting."²³ The essence of such meeting is subjectivity, I and Thou meeting, the whole being speaking in the primary word, I and Thou, not in the secondary, objective sense making the Thou into an It.²⁴ In religious understanding God addresses each, and each responds to God, not as an It or object, but as the Thou, or subject. In relational discourse between two human subjects, their I and Thou can become the context for the divine Thou to be heard and answered. This would fulfill Jesus' promise, "where two or three are gathered in my name, I am there among them" (Matthew 18:20).

This does not mean that God is never an It, an object. Theology necessarily makes God an It with believers in an I-It relationship to the Ultimate One. We try to express our understanding *about* God to one another. Often, out of that theological framework, say in preaching, or teaching, or sharing with one or two or a few, the I-Thou of existential discourse takes place: the whole being speaking the primary word I-Thou.²⁵

This is the essence of what Kierkegaard so clearly symbolized in his suggestive use of theater: In worship, the preacher is the prompter whispering in the wings; God is the audience (i.e. auditor) listening to the lines spoken and how they are heard; and each congregant is the actor who acts before God. The action is each responding with the total self to the Thou who has already spoken and is joining each to hear the response of faith from each.²⁶ The preacher is directly involved in the I-Thou discourse, responding to the divine Thou even as he or she prompts others as actors to respond to the Word of God. So Calvin's "right hearing of the Word" is given even deeper, richer meaning by Kierkegaard and Buber: in every discourse the Divine Thou is speaking to, and listening to, each self as that self meets God with the whole response in the mode of I-Thou. Ronald Gregor Smith has called this I-Thou meeting the mysticism "of real communion with God."²⁷ "I meet the Other."²⁸

Through preaching do we hear the call of Being Itself to our being with sufficient clarity for us to be called upon to answer? That is partly the task of the preacher, partly the task of the hearer, partly the task of the Holy Spirit. Preaching is articulating in the preacher's own responsive way the vision of the saving Reality that grasped her or him. And the hearer's response is her or his response to that vision. The Holy Spirit's role is to help make alive the vision. God aims toward each for each in her or his actualizing moment: the moment for the divine/human meeting.

William Alston in his *Philosophy of Language* sees language as a "calling to mind."²⁹ That is exactly what preaching, teaching as in church school classes, sharing as in support groups, family grace and prayers, and one-to-one relationships, and so on, do, or should do; that is, call to mind. But "calling to mind" presupposes a deposit of memories in the mind to which the linguistic signs and symbols refer. How crucial it is to have some Christian/theological/biblical base to which language appeals. The total actualized past prehended, or emotionally felt, is continued in the stream or duration of constant becoming. When the past with its billions of events and the future with its vast but relevant lure of possibilities inform the actualizing moment as each must make response in putting together this existential moment, the linguistic symbol uttered and heard can be used by God to prompt a "decision" toward the increase of the love of God and neighbor in the world, which is what the church as the storer, the deliverer, the shaper of today toward tomorrow is all about. Alston has written that meaningfulness depends on expression that connects with the intuitions of the community being addressed.³⁰

Expressions become meaningful if they elicit in us an idea or a feeling or a memory; that is, if they connect with, or lift up, something in the rich memory track loaded with our past. New experiences in the present become part of that track for future occasions of becoming, whether two minutes from now or two years. The church is a community of experience and meaning. Its linguistic and other symbolic expressions lift that community's memory into new prominence as they nest each of us in the intuitions of our past experience and help us to elicit from those intuitions a new response to the creative urging of God. Language elicits feeling that has within it the whole duration of the person hearing, experiencing, responding. For example, aspects in the life of Jesus: the baby, the mother, the manger straw, the life lived out in self-giving, forgiving, servanthood; the death with its pain but its continuing loving concerns; these are part of our own prehended past out of homes, church school, worship, and so forth. Language elicits feeling that has within it the whole duration and helps aim the soul's intention toward a richer novelty guided by the tender leading of God.

The ability to hear as well as speak (and sign language includes both dimensions) the language of faith is essential to every form of ministry, lay as well as professional. In our study of how faith is formed,[31] the majority of the laypeople interviewed expressed deep regret that they did not have a sufficient grasp of the language of the Christian faith in which to hear and express their faith. They expressed a sense of deprivation: that they could not enter into dialogue in any depth within their own church. They probably could not have put their feelings in Buber's "I and Thou" terms, but they were expressing their feelings of loss within the community of faith. Linguistic expression is a crucial mode of consciousness, as I have tried to urge in this chapter. If ministry is the response of faithful people to work with the God who addresses us to create something of beauty in each moment of becoming, every effort on the part of the specially trained professionals in ministry to help assist each to enrich her or his facility with the language of faith will be to work with God toward the ultimate goal of the church: to increase the love of God and neighbor in the world. Such enrichment will be a move toward what Whitehead said we must ask of theology, "to express that element in perishing lives which is undying by reason of its expression of perfections proper to our finite natures. In this way we shall understand how life includes a mode of satisfaction deeper than joy or sorrow."[32]

In our next chapter we shall look at spirituality as the thing of beauty. It is spirituality that is the ultimate perfection "proper to our finite natures." Perhaps with no other theological subject—unless it be prayer, which, as we shall see, is essential to spirituality—is there more unclarity than around spirituality among the people of God, professional and non-professional. It would seem that men and women who are the professionally educated ministers have no more pressing need than to clarify linguistically what spirituality is and how it comes about so that more richly informed lay ministers can help create spirituality in the church and in the world. To that we turn in our closing chapter.

9

Spirituality: The Thing of Beauty

Spirit refers to the radically self-transcending character of human existence...Spiritual existence expresses itself in love.
John B. Cobb, Jr.

The aim of life, at the human level, is to create people of greater stature.
Bernard Loomer

Building on the process model of what reality looks like, which is the substance of the first four chapters, and employing the modes of importance, intentionality, imagination, and linguistic expression developed in the next four chapters, we come to the thing of beauty that every form of ministry, whether professional or lay, should have as its primary goal: spirituality.

At the outset we must define or identify what we mean by the very vague word *spirituality*. With this identifying of spirituality Paul Tillich is very helpful. He makes the careful distinction between "preliminary concerns" and "ultimate concern." While this distinction is drawn in his defining theology, the distinction is essential to spirituality. Every moment we human beings are involved in preliminary concerns: homemaking, business operations, entertainment and leisure activities, schooling, neighborly relations, and so forth. Spirituality, or "religious concern," is ultimate, unconditional, with "no part of ourselves or of our world" excluded. It is inclusive of preliminary concerns, but it is "ultimate, unconditional, total, and infinite." Tillich puts it biblically: "Ultimate concern is the abstract translation of the great commandment: 'The Lord, our God, the Lord is one; and you shall love the Lord your God with all your heart, and with all your soul and with all your mind, and with all your strength (Mark 12:29).'"[1]

Spirituality is not set over against body, or heart, or mind. Rather, it is inclusive of the total person, the divine Spirit coming together with the human spirit reaching for ultimacy. Spirit is the life of the soul, but not over against body and mind. "It is the all-embracing function in which all elements of the structure of being [body, mind, soul] participate. Spirit is the inclusive symbol."[2]

Spirituality is not the human being standing on tiptoe. The human being is a sinner, for example, so often making preliminary concerns into some form of ultimacy. This is the essence of idolatry. But the human being, especially as represented in soul as nephesh, is groping for or toward transcendence. The infinite Spirit (ruah) searches for, finds, seizes hold on the human spirit, a term summarizing the whole being, and lifts it toward ultimacy, that is, toward its created position of imaging God, fulfilling its ultimate relationship as next of kin with God. But this ultimacy as spirituality is not divorced from the temporal flux. Tillich agrees with Bergson, who combined the elan vital, the universal tendency toward self-transcendence, with duration, with continuity and self-conservation in the flow of time.[3]

Within the metaphysical vision of process, the human being is spiritual when she or he is most truly imitating the everlasting Creator.⁴ This imitating of God is faith walking in grace; grace empowering each toward the love of God, of the neighbor, of the self. Thus, the abstract becomes concrete; the search for beauty is actualized for the moment, the moment made possible by the divine Artist as it is concretized in the concrescence of past and possibility.

Spirituality resides in this biblical directive: "Strive first for the kingdom of God and his righteousness" (Matthew 6:33). This spiritual seeking does not negate or ignore everyday concerns about what to eat, or drink, or wear, all important but preliminary concerns. Jesus assures his listeners that all these things shall be theirs as well. Kierkegaard put it so pithily: "Purity of heart is to will one thing."⁵

Spirituality is the intentionality of each of us to focus on what God wants, to will that, to be "oned with God," and all the rest of our intentions can then be brought into that focus. As Daniel Day Williams put it, "It is possible for human beings, in response to the power and goodness of God, to begin to will His Kingdom above all other things and to grow toward a more mature expression of that will."⁶ Thus, while we do not possess, nor are we possessed by, love as we respond to the grace of God, yet a "beginning of a response in love to the grace of God is possible and growth in grace as a maturing in that life is possible."⁷

What Williams is talking about in these challenging words is the "pilgrimage of the human spirit."⁸ There is in the metaphysical doctrine of process the real possibility of growth into, and in, spirituality. Of course, growth in the life of the spirit, guided by the Spirit of God, brings new temptations with it, the chief of which may be spiritual pride or self-righteousness, a false complacency, a heavy dogmatism, to name but three. But in the pilgrimage of the human spirit, progress in the capacity to love shows itself in deeper appreciation for, and empathy toward, others, more self-giving, more care or concern for dealing skillfully with human problems, e.g., the environment, and more maturity with regard to our attachments to the goods of our earthly existence.[9]

But spirituality, as conceived in the process model, is fundamentally a new dedication or commitment of the whole self to the working of God in each of us and among us. And at least in the Christian community it is clear what this working looks like. Whitehead ascribed to Plato the insight that the divine element in the world is to be conceived as persuasive energy. But he saw in the life of Christ the demonstration of Plato's insight. It is important to let Whitehead describe what the "supreme moment in religious history, according to the Christian religion," revealed:

> The essence of Christianity is the appeal to the life of Christ as a revelation of the nature of God and of his agency in the world. The record is fragmentary, inconsistent and uncertain…But there can be no doubt as to what elements in the record have evoked a response from all that is best in human nature. The Mother, the Child, and the bare manger: The lowly man, homeless and self-forgetful, with his message of peace, love, and sympathy: the suffering, the agony, the tender words as life ebbed, the final despair: and the whole with the authority of supreme victory.
>
> I need not elaborate. Can there be any doubt that the power of Christianity lies in its revelation in act, of that which Plato divined in theory?[10]

Spirituality is no arrival at a destination. Rather, it is the total human self—body, mind, soul—responding to the creative working of God instant by instant, so that "brute process" is infused with "tenderness, meaning, and beauty."[11] Spirituality is adventuring. It means to adventure beyond, to aspire beyond my present desires, wants, and achievements. It is a gentle dissatisfaction with what is, reaching toward some transcendent vision, not elusive but graspable, because God makes it possible.

The model is the revelation in the person of Jesus of Nazareth of who God is, what God is like, what God requires of us; and the active presence of God, the divine Spirit, who makes possible the adventure called love. As Paul so succinctly told the church at Corinth: "God was in Christ reconciling the world to himself, not counting their trespasses against them (2 Corinthians 5:19). In the very human Jesus, God incarnated the divine Self, telling and showing the world the meaning of love. The Word of God, meaning the very essence of God, became flesh and dwelt among us. Living with this Jesus Christ, the embodied Word, listening to his teaching, painfully watching him die as he heard him cry out, "My God, my God, why have you forsaken me?" (Mark. 15:34); and then in the utter act of faith, "Father, into your hands I commend my spirit" (Luke 23:46), the disciple John knew "God is love." (1 John 4:8).

For the Christian community, at least, spirituality is to live after the manner of Jesus, who was part and parcel of our very human situation, for as Paul also theologized, "For our sake he made him to be sin who knew no sin, so that in him we might become the righteousness of God" (2 Corinthians 5:21). We are forgiven: the consummate act of love! As John Cobb has written of this love, "Love is…on the one hand, the only salvation of the spiritual person and, on the other hand, unattainable by his own efforts."[12] The human being is self-centered, self-preoccupied (a form of spiritual pride), rebellious against God, and guilty of injustice toward the neighbor.[13] At the core of sin is pride. This can be intellectual pride, moral pride, lusting for power as in greed, and ultimately spiritual pride.[14] So spirituality, the thing of beauty we are intended for as our souls are transcendently hungry and eager for God, is sinfully turned back on itself, curving in and around itself, which is the sheer ugliness of sin. But we are forgiven: the divine Being taking into the divine Self incarnated in Christ our arrogance, our pride, our shaking of our fists in the face of God, thereby saying, "We'll see who's boss!" Such is God's love that what we cannot attain, God in Christ has attained for us. Cobb pinpoints spirituality in love: "We love only because we are first loved. In this way, and only in this way, can the spiritual person genuinely and purely love."[15] Sin forgiven; the anxiety of our finitude is at least partly overcome; yet we can love because God first loved us. As John wrote: "In this is love, not that we loved God but that He loved us and sent His Son to be the atoning sacrifice for our sins. Beloved, since God loved us so much, we also ought to love one another" (1 John 4:10–11).

Lewis Smedes picked this up in these apt words describing the woman who was a sinner who wet Jesus' feet with her tears, wiped them with her hair, kissed his feet, and anointed them with ointment: "She loves much because she has been forgiven much"—this was Jesus' explanation for a woman who dared to barge into a dinner party uninvited, plunk herself at Jesus' feet, and pour out a small cascade of love."[16] This is spirituality, a moment of beauty, in which a forgiven human being responded in an act of love as the divine Spirit and hers met to form a moment of shalom. Is this not what ministry, whether clergy or lay, is all about: in an act of love creating a thing of beauty?

Briefly let us picture three stages in life's journey as Erik Erikson has brilliantly analyzed them, to see what beauty might be possible as we minister to children in the oedipal stage, to adolescents in their search for identity, and to adults in the midlife crisis stage of human development.

Erikson's third stage of human development is initiative vs. guilt, covering the ages roughly from four to six.[17] This is the phallic period for the boy, in Freud's terminology the oedipus complex, which also has sexual meaning for the girl. The child has possessive attachment to the parent of the opposite sex. This attachment of the boy toward his mother and the girl toward her father involves sibling rivalry, anxiety born of guilt and fear, especially for the boy because of castration anxiety, and even jealousies of parental affection for each other. This period in the child's life is marked by the intrusive mode of vigorous locomotion into space, aggressive talk, either real or feigned attacks on other bodies, a consuming curiosity, and the opening up of the imagination, which may frighten the child.[18] Small wonder that Franz Alexander can write: "Childhood is the most vulnerable phase of human development. Bad educational or traumatic experiences of any kind which may increase this conflict exert a pathogenic influence upon later life."[19] As Erikson shows, the danger of this initiative stage is guilt.[20] This is the essential meaning of the castration complex: Potential destruction attaches to the oedipal fantasies. The child becomes divided, which is his or her sense of guilt, coming at the same time that the driving initiative of this period directs the child. There may be, and probably will be in these formative years, "resignation, guilt, and anxiety." Masturbation, especially with the boy, occurs during this period with the reaction of parents often producing guilt feelings and fear of loss of genitals. Erikson observes that the girl is "apt to develop, together with the basic modes of feminine *inception* and maternal *inclusion*, either a teasing, demanding, grasping attitude, which at its height becomes what is called bitchiness or a clinging and overly dependent childishness."[21] But the prerequisites for initiative, that is, for the "selection of goals and perseverance in approaching them," are also dynamically present in this third stage of life.

Before we ask what ministry has to do with this very formative stage, we need to look briefly at basic human needs as set forth by Abraham Maslow.[22] He lists five basic needs, and while he does not equate them with any stage of development, as "basic needs" they are relevant to all stages; they help us to see what needs must be satisfied if initiative is to proceed in the four-, five-, and six-year-old, with guilt being reduced. Maslow's basic needs start from the more elemental and move upward toward higher and higher potentiality. The needs are: (1) physiological, e.g., hunger; (2) safety, i.e., an orderly, predictable world the average child wants; (3) belongingness and love, i.e., affection both received and given; (4) esteem, i.e., a firm, stable self-respect; (5) self-actualization, i.e. doing what one is fitted for. For the child in the third stage of development the beginning of the satiation of these five needs is essential to appropriate initiative. While self-actualization is the fifth need, it should not be seen as applicable only to later or adult years. Initiative as used by Erikson and self-actualization as used by Maslow apply to Erikson's third stage. Ministry, as I am using the term, is extremely important to help the child in this stage toward self-actualization appropriate to this age. This ministry should be characteristic of church school education for preschoolers, of day-care centers, of home life, of neighborhood relationships.

One model for such ministry is Mister Rogers Neighborhood. Fred Rogers, a Presbyterian clergy, practices his ministry by way of the television screen, to be sure, but his practice, geared to all children, is so perfectly appropriate to encouraging initiative and self-actualization. This, of course, is partly due to the mentoring of his dear friend, Dr. Margaret McFarland, a fellow worker with Erik Erikson in his research in Pittsburgh. When Fred Rogers sings his famous lines to children through the medium of television, "I like you just the way you are," "And you're important just the way you are," he is building in them trust and self-esteem. He is dealing with fears, questions, the kinds of things children of this age deal with, which most adults do not understand at the child's level. It takes time, forethought, patience, genuine concern on the part of the adult to have the mind of the child in his or her existential situation. Fred Rogers' ministry is to help the child actualize himself or herself toward self-transcendency, that is, toward a new height in the next moment of his or her becoming. Of course, he gets to this building of self-esteem by way of art: puppets and song, for example, to express the needs, the desires, the fears, the questions, the anger, the jealousy, the aggression, the egotism that kids are experiencing. He also uses adults to enhance his message to the children.

While church school teachers, parents, pre-school carers, and neighborhood models may not have the insights, the empathy, or the artistic capabilities of Fred Rogers, they as ministers have the calling to help create the children struggling to become something of beauty. Communicating love—"I like you just the way you are"—phrased in word, smile, gentle hands and arms, is the possibility and the responsibility of each of us shaping the lives of children into a spirituality appropriate to their ages. The actualized past of these children then becomes rich data for their adolescent and adult years as they help to process their lives toward the possibilities by which the divine Spirit is luring them. That luring is the gentle Spirit's creative guidance toward fulfilling all that they can become in each moment, which is the essence of spirituality.

We shall skip Erikson's fourth stage of latency and look at adolescence, which Erikson describes as the stage of identity vs. role diffusion. The word adolescence, from the Latin *adolesco*, means to grow up, come to maturity, ripen. The adolescent lives in a "no man's land" between the protected dependency of childhood and the relatively independent world of the adult. In this land youth is struggling for ego identity: Who am I? The identity struggle is sexual, with and over against the opposite sex; vocational, as one anticipates and prepares for the world of work; social, as the young person checks his or her meaning for others, tries to find a group or clique where there is some comfort, and latches on to heroes in the world of sports, music, theater, and so on; philosophical, as one struggles for ideas, values, meanings, in which religion should be able to play a major role if it is a living, active, even daring concept and a challenge to coincide with the dynamism of this decisive period of growth and change. The adolescents are in the painful process of sorting out their loves and hates, which is another way of saying they are trying to locate their own discrete identity. This is a vivid but not necessarily a happy time.

The danger in this stage is role diffusion. Erikson argues that primarily the inability to settle on an occupational identity leads to role diffusion in the adolescent.[23] He or she, in struggling toward what the self wants to be, can be, should be, especially in the work world, often tries to prove or substantiate the self with gangs, drinking, leaving school, with the opposite sex, and so forth. With identity very unclear, role diffusion leaves the young person moody, unpredictable, erratic, capable of great mood swings. So adolescence is a painful process in this climactic growing-up time. But this role searching, including the diffusion almost inevitably involved, can often be the locus for ideology as the adolescent is intellectually, socially, vocationally struggling for self-identity. As Erikson has written about the youth who has not come to some resolution of his or her "identity crisis": "the adolescent mind becomes a more explicitly ideological one, by which we mean one searching for some inspiring unification of tradition or anticipated techniques, ideas, and ideals. And, indeed, it is the ideological potential of a society which speaks most clearly to the adolescent who is so eager to be affirmed by peers, to be confirmed by teachers, and to be inspired by worth-while 'ways of life.'"[24]

Those who minister to youth, not in the professional sense of ministry but in the relational sense of serving, have much to offer by modeling and talking, without "preaching," of "worthwhile ways of life." These include all parents and other adult family members, neighbors, schoolteachers, coaches, group leaders as in Scouting, and Rainbow, as well as church school teachers, youth advisors, camp directors, choir directors, and so on. There is no substitute for close, individual relationships between pastors and their young people. When the young person becomes aware that the pastor cares empathically, is there when the fifteen-year-old really needs that caring, feels the love as the

Spirituality: The Thing of Beauty 111

pastor helps him or her to prepare to read a scripture lesson in the worship service, the young person may well be opened to a level of spirituality in which his or her total self is opened up to a leading that can create a moment, a series of moments, a life direction toward beauty. Youth is a daring stage, a stage of movement; and building on the basic psychological need for identity, ministry that helps to build self-esteem in adolescence can be a partner with the divine in creating a spirituality that can continue to grow, yes, to blossom, into the next stages of life.

In concluding this chapter, we shall move to the seventh stage Erikson identified: generativity vs. stagnation. Only we shall view this stage as the midlife crisis stage. Daniel Levinson and his group of researchers studying the adult life cycle isolate four polarities in which the male is involved: young/old, masculine/feminine, destructive/creative, attached/separate.[25] However, females are as involved in this polarity as males and, therefore, Levinson shows the need for movement toward balance: the male toward need fulfilment of nurturance and dependency, the female toward assertive and aggressive inclinations, such psychosocial movement appearing to be a task of middle age.[26] If the male's movement toward the rich inclusion of his feminine side is initiated, he might fulfill Erikson's description of generativity in his midlife; if not, the polarity of stagnation. But if the male cannot come to grips with his feminine side for any number of reasons, e.g., threat of homophobia, threatened loss of manhood as society defines it, premature sign of aging (thus seizing the pole of young and rejecting the inclusion of the pole of old), then stagnation would characterize this stage for the male. Or the female confronted by the "empty nest syndrome," facing a future without her identity as mother as she has known it, and asking herself whether she is content to be "just" his wife and tending to household chores, or whether she will go back to school and begin a career (with or without his support), can move to a new level of generativity, such as "developing a feeling of responsibility to the community."[27] But a failure for the woman to make this kind of move, for whatever reason, may lock her into stagnation with its boredom, loss of vitality, and the possibility of suicide because of meaninglessness. Stagnation, whether in the male or female, fulfills Jung's definition of neurosis: "an inner cleavage—the state of being at war with oneself."[28]

Is there a much sadder sight than a person somewhere between thirty-five and fifty-five who has leveled off, settled in, become encapsulated, bound, constricted? Carl Jung claimed that about a third of his cases were "suffering from no clinically definable neurosis, but from the senselessness and emptiness of their lives." He calls this state the "general neurosis of our time."[29] Is this Kierkegaard's person who prefers living in the basement? A person forty years of age has prehended the varied data of his or her past in well over thirteen billion events, a massive process of constant emerging. In those billions of events God has been bringing new possibilities to bear on that forty-year-old, event after event. Constantly that human has been aiming his or her life toward goals, provided by both the accumulation of forty years and by God. In each tenth of a second, let us say, he or she has had to constitute the self, become something, put it all together to add one more events to world history as well as personal history. But if that person has become stagnated, in that life there are narrow commitments, narrow allegiances, narrow vision. There are few contrasts to open up that life, practically no transcending vision. It is a midlife of stagnation, an ugly life, a sad life, a life that is dehumanized. And perhaps this mid-life person feels no pain at all. Here is Sartre's *en soi* human being with few adventures, few goals, no overarching projects or projections, only repetition. Here is T. S. Eliot's Prufrock, who wonders,

> Do I dare
> Disturb the universe?...
> I have measured out my life with coffee spoons...
> I have seen the moment of my greatness flicker,

And I have seen the eternal Footman hold my coat, and snicker,
And in short, I was afraid.³⁰

Here is Albert Camus' lawyer in *The Fall*, Jean-Baptiste Clemence, whose life revolves around his unabsolved guilt. While he longs for the purity of fallen snow, he knows it's fleeting before tomorrow's mud. For a woman threw herself into the Seine and he walked on by, never risking his life. For years he has wanted to utter the words that echoed through his nights: "O young woman, throw yourself into the water again so that I may a second time have the chance of saving both of us!...Brr...! The water's so cold! But let's not worry! It's too late now. It will always be too late. Fortunately!"³¹

In the inner wrestle Jean Baptiste's aim is narrow: self-protection, despite the pain of guilt and the anguish of cowardice. It is the existential moment: the self aborning, struggling to actualize itself between past and future, between what has been and what might be, struggling to gain a new self, but locked into the evil: "too late." Prufrock, afraid to seize the moment, will continue to measure out his life with coffee spoons. Lives enacted in Jean Baptiste and Prufrock are tragic lives needing desperately the radically transcending character of spiritual existence, which is a further development of personal existence.

John B. Cobb, Jr., whose term "spiritual existence" I am using, argues that this is possible by way of living from the initiative of God. Cobb sees this spiritual existence as expressing itself in love.³² The essential function of ministry is to be with the Jean Baptistes and Purfrocks of this world in love so that they might in turn be with others as carers who can be instruments of God to create a thing of beauty, spiritual existence, in their lives. What is this love? It is the very human love drive, eros, reborn of the divine love drive, agape, and empowered by that love. This agapized eros enables sinful eros to move to the side of others and remain there faithfully and provides perspective for the other's potential humanness to be seen and encouraged. It is this love that bequeaths hope, faith, love. This divine love fills human eros so that we are liberated and can afford to be free. In this freedom we can stand with others to share gently with them what we have received: the gift of God's love, graciously tendered by God. We can then become with others a community that is empathic and supportive, a community that knows it is forgiven and can therefore afford to give; a community of Socratic midwives at work creating with the divine Creator children, youth, adults toward the vision God has for each to become.

Perhaps a model is Johann von Staupitz, Vicar-General of the Augustinian order in Germany, who became a co-creator, with God, of the young man, Martin Luther. Young Luther had no hope, was tormented by his lifelong antagonist, the devil, was angry with God, whom he felt was angry with him for "my sin, my sin, my sin." Von Staupitz helped Luther to see and believe that God was merciful and forgiving. "Gradually, under Staupitz's tutelage, his eyes were opened, and a new gospel dawned upon his gaze."[33]

While our destiny is not for all to become a Luther, it is the calling of each to become a Staupitz. I am talking about the calling of each of us to be ministers who will hear, listen, pay attention to the persuasive word of God coming in effective love-power to participate with God to create a thing of beauty. As we have already seen, Whitehead envisages God as "the poet of the world, with tender patience leading it by his vision of truth, beauty, and goodness."[34] The ministry of all God's people is to participate with God in creating beauty, which obviously includes truth and goodness. "Creation is an art," as Meland has poeticized, "and God is one who works the artist's way."[35] What higher calling for the people of God can there be than to be guided by the divine Poet who ceaselessly labors to create souls of beauty!

Souls of beauty are shalom souls, souls that have some experience of the peace, the harmony, the wholeness from God that they have actualized, and are in the process of actualizing, in their moment-by-moment becoming. Shalom souls are experiencing a covenant of harmony, harmony within and harmony in all relationships. As we saw in chapter 4, there is no static or completed arrival of the shalom soul, as though one had achieved his or her goal or arrived at a goal. Rather, the shalom soul is the soul struggling through and beyond penultimate ends, so dominant in our human fragmented cultures and especially in our consumer, individualistic, economically driven set of goals, toward the ultimate vision of what God is striving to create in each of us along the journeying of our lives.

Christians as ministers are God's messengers, servants, midwives called by God to help enable the divine vision to become actualized as shalom events in a child, an adolescent, an adult of any age. Thus, love of God and neighbor can be realized in the world, moment by moment, as God uses the medium of faithful people to help create shalom experiences. And the cosmic Artist's vision of beauty can now and then be realized: the covenantal kingdom experience. Ministry is a rich assignment and a glorious calling: to become artists pursuing the Galilean vision.

Notes

Chapter 1

[1] For an analysis of these three forms of faith see Gordon E. Jackson with Phyllisee Foust Jackson, *Pathways to Faith* (Nashville: Abingdon Press, 1989), ch. 1.

[2] See Henri Bergson, *Time and Free Will* (New York: Harper, 1960), ch.2.

[3] Alfred North Whitehead, *Process and Reality* (New York: Macmillan, 1929), p. 123.

[4] On causal efficacy see Alfred North Whitehead, *Process and Reality*, ch. VIII; Alfred North Whitehead, *Adventures of Ideas* (New York: Macmillan, 1933), Part III, *passim*; John B. Cobb, Jr., *A Christian Natural Theology* (Philadelphia: Westminster, 1985), p. 28ff.

[5] Cf. Whitehead, *Process and Reality*, p. 250.

[6] Whitehead, *Adventures of Ideas* (New York: Macmillan, 1933), p. 210.

[7] Whitehead, *Modes of Thought* (New York: Macmillan, 1938), p. 121.

[8] Whitehead, *Process and Reality*, p. 73.

[9] Whitehead, *Process and Reality*, p. 526.

[10] Ibid., p. 532.

[11] Freud, also, distinguished dread from fear. See his *Introductory Lecures on Psychoanalysis*, ch. 25; and *The Problem of Anxiety*, ch. 8.

[12] Martin Heidegger, *Being and Time*, pp. 238, 239.

[13] Whitehead, *Adventures of Ideas* (New York: The Free Press, 1933), p. 176.

[14] Whitehead, *Modes of Thought* (New York: Capricorn Books, 1938), p. 228.

Chapter 2

[1] Paul D. MacLean, *The Triune Brain in Evolution* (New York and London: Plenum Press, 1990.)

[2] MacLean, p. 568.

[3] MacLean, p. 234.

[4] See Sigmund Freud, *Beyond the Pleasure Principle*, tr. by James Strachey (New York; Bantam).

[5] MacLean, p. 231.

[6] Cf. Carl Sagan, *The Dragons of Eden* (New York: Ballantine Books, 1977), p.82.

[7] MacLean, p. 237.

[8] William Barrett, *Irrational Man* (New York: Doubleday Anchor Books, 1962) p. 135.

[9] MacLean, pp. 237, 238.

[10] MacLean, p. 243.

[11] Ibid.

[12] Ibid.

[13] Richard M. Restak, *The Brain: The Last Frontier* (Garden City: Doubleday, 1979), p. 37.

[14] Ibid., p. 37.

[15] Ibid., p. 46.

[16] Ibid., p. 58; cf. 382.

[17] MacLean, p. 437ff.
[18] Karen Horney, *Neurotic Personality of Our Time* (New York: Norton, 1937).
[19] MacLean, pp. 247, 445f.
[20] MacLean, pp. 397ff.
[21] MacLean, p. 465.
[22] Cf. Restak, pp. 63, 64.
[23] MacLean, p. 543ff.
[24] Cf. Carl Sagan, *The Dragons of Eden*, passim.
[25] Cf. Restak, p. 27.
[26] Cf. MacLean, pp. 520, 534.
[27] MacLean, p. 559.
[28] MacLean, p. 569.
[29] MacLean, p. 579.
[30] Restak, p. 30.
[31] Sagan, p. 62. (Carl Sagan wonders: "Does the metaphor of the serpent [in Genesis 3] refer to the use of the aggressive and ritualistic reptilian component of our brain in the further evolution of the neocortex?" (p. 150).
[32] Sagan, p. 248.
[33] C. G. Jung, *The Archetypes and the Collective Unconscious*, tr. R. F. C. Hull (London: Routledge and Kegan Paul, 1959), The Collected Works, vol. 9, part I, pp. 3, 4, 42ff.
[34] Cf. Ibid., I.
[35] Cf. ibid, p. 5; Joseph Campbell, *The Power of Myth* (New York: Doubleday, 1988), p. 51.
[36] C.G. Jung, *Two Essays on Analytical Psychology*, tr. R. F. C. Hull (London: Routledge and Kegan Paul, 1953), Collected Works, vol. 7, p. 188.
[37] Frieda Fordham, *An Introduction to Jung's Psychology* (Baltimore: Penguin, 1959), p. 53.
[38] C. G. Jung, *Aion*, tr. R. F. C. Hull (London: Routledge and Kegan Paul, 1959), Collected Works, vol. 9, Part II, p. 13.
[39] C. H. Dodd, *The Epistle of Paul to the Romans* (New York: Harper, n.d.) p. 107.
[40] Rudolf Bultmann, *Theology of the New Testament* (New York: Scribner, 1951), I, p. 245.
[41] Paul Ricoeur, *The Symbolism of Evil* (Boston: Beacon, 1967), tr. Emerson Buchanan, p. 50.
[42] Ibid., p. 51.
[43] Johannes Pedersen, *Israel: Its Life and Culture I–II* (London: Oxford, 1926), p. 415.
[44] Ricoeur, p. 51.
[45] Søren Kierkegaard, *The Sickness unto Death* (Princeton: Princeton University Press, 1946), tr. Walter Lawrie. Cf. Paul Tillich, *The Courage To Be* (New Haven: Yale University Press, 1952), ch. 2.
[46] Emil Brunner, *Man in Revolt* (Philadelphia: Westminster Press, 1947), p. 132.
[47] Cf. Kierkegaard, *The Sickness unto Death*, passim.
[48] Nietzsche's insight albeit his faulty logic: "If there were a God who could bear not to be God. Therefore, there is no God."
[49] Reinhold Niebuhr, *The Nature and Destiny of Man* (New York: Scribner, 1943), I, pp. 178,179,192.

⁵⁰Romans 6:12.
⁵¹Sagan, *Dragons of Eden*, pp. 45, 46.
⁵²Ibid., p. 168.
⁵³Whitehead, *Adventures of Ideas*, p. 213.

Chapter 3

¹Charles Hartshorne, *Man's Vision of God* (Chicago: Willett, Clark, 1941), p. 16f.
²Whitehead, *Adventures of Ideas*, pp. 160, 166.
³Ibid., p. 167.
⁴Whitehead, *Process and Reality*, p. 520.
⁵Whitehead, *Religion in the Making*, p. 153.
⁶Ibid., p. 155.
⁷Whitehead, *Adventures of Ideas*, p. 169.
⁸Bernard Meland, *The Reawakening of Christian Faith* (New York: Macmillan, 1949), p. 100.
⁹Ibid., p. 118.
¹⁰Whitehead, *Religion in the Making*, p. 159.
¹¹Ibid., pp. 159, 156.
¹²Whitehead, *Process and Reality*, p. 532.
¹³Ibid., p. 533.
¹⁴Ibid., p. 528.
¹⁵Charles Hartshorne, "Tillich's Doctrine of God," in Charles W. Kegley and Robert W. Bretall, *The Theology of Paul Tillich* (New York: Macmillan, 1952), p. 192.
¹⁶Whitehead, *Modes of Thought*, p. 141.
¹⁷Hartshorne, *Man's Vision of God*, p. 294. Emphasis is Hartshorne's.
¹⁸Whitehead, *Modes of Thought*, p. 140.
¹⁹Hartshorne, *Man's Vision of God*, p. 212.
²⁰Ibid., p. 216.
²¹Whitehead, *Religion in the Making*, p. 105.
²²Ibid., p. 158f.
²³Meland, *Seeds of Redemption*, p. 60.

Chapter 4

¹Jack L. Stotts, *Shalom: The Search for a Peaceable City* (Nashville: Abingdon, 1973), p. 97. Teran-Dutari's article "Peace" is found in *Sacramentum Mundi: An Encyclopaedia of Theology*, ed. Karl Rahner (London: Burns and Oates, 1969), IV, 380.
²Stotts, *Shalom.*, p. 98.
³Johannes Pedersen, *Israel: Its Life and Culture* (London: Oxford University Press, 1940), I–II, 285 and III-IV, 359.
⁴Ibid., I–II, 311.
⁵Thomas Hobbes, *Leviathan* (Oxford: Blackwell, 1960), ch. 13.
⁶Reinhold Niebuhr, *The Nature and Destiny of Man* (New York: Scribner's, 1943), I, ch. VII.
⁷William Barrett, *Irrational Man* (Garden City: Doubleday Anchor, 1958), p. 138.
⁸Pedersen, III–IV, p. 612.
⁹Stotts, *Shalom,* p. 98.

[10] Ibid., p. 100.
[11] Ibid., p. 104.
[12] Douglas Sturm, *Community and Alienation Essays on Process Thought and Public Life* (Notre Dame: University of Notre Dame Press, 1988), p. 203.
[13] Pedersen, *Israel*, I-II, pp. 287, 297.
[14] Stotts, *Shalom*, p. 110.
[15] Cf. John Macquarrie, *The Concept of Peace* (London: SCM Press, 1923), p. 358ff.
[16] Donald E. Gowan, *Shalom: A Study of the Biblical Concept of Peace* (Pittsburgh: The Kerygma Program, 1984), p. 12.
[17] Meland, *Seeds of Redemption*, p. 69.
[18] Ibid., p. 69.
[19] Paul Tillich, *Systematic Theology* (Chicago: University of Chicago Press), I, pp. 4, 5.
[20] Meland, *Seeds of Redemption*, p. 59.
[21] Ibid., pp. 59,60.
[22] Norman Pittenger, *God in Process* (London: SCM Press, 1967), p. 22.
[23] Whitehead, *Process and Reality*, p. 532.
[24] Meland, *Seeds of Redemption*, pp. 68, 70.
[25] Whitehead, *Process and Reality*, p. 427.

Chapter 5

[1] William James, *Pragmatism* (Meridian Books, 1955), p. 134.
[2] Gustav Gluck, *Peter Bruegel The Elder* (Paris: The Hyperion Press, 1936), p. 28.
[3] Cf. Douglas Sturm, *Community and Alienation: Essays On Process Thought and Public Life*; John Rawls, *A Theory of Justice* (Cambridge, Mass.: The Belknap Press of Harvard University Press, 1971); M. Douglas Meeks, *God the Economist* (Minneapolis: Fortress Press, 1989).
[4] *Modes of Thought*, p. 70.
[5] David Ray Griffin, *God and Religion in the Postmodern World* (Albany: State University of New York Press, 1989), p. 13.
[6] Whitehead, *Modes of Thought*, p. 28.
[7] *Process and Reality*, p. 532.
[8] Ibid.
[9] John Calvin, *Institutes of the Christian Religion* (Philadelphia: Presbyterian Board of Christian Education, n.d.), I, Bk.1, p. 218.
[10] Ibid., Bk.16, p. 217.
[11] Meland, *Seeds of Redemption*, p. 82.
[12] Blaise Pascal, *Pensées* (New York: Modern Library, 1941), p. 95.
[13] Howard Thurman, *Disciplines of the Spirit* (New York: Harper, 1963), p. 87.
[14] Thomas Merton, *Contemplative Prayer* (Garden City: Image, 1971), p. 67.
[15] *Rufus Jones Speaks to Our Time: An Anthology* ed. Harry Emerson Fosdick (New York: Macmillan, 1951), p. 155.
[16] Harry Emerson Fosdick, *The Three Meanings: Prayer, Faith, Service* (Garden City: Garden City Books, 1951), p. 34.
[17] Ibid., p. 142.
[18] Gordon E. Jackson with Phyllisee F. Jackson, *Pathways to Faith*, ch. 6.
[19] William James, *The Varieties of Religious Experience* (New York: Modern Library, 1902), p. 467.

²⁰Ibid., p. 454.
²¹Ibid.
²²Henri J. Nouwen, *The Wounded Healer* (New York: Doubleday, 1972), p. 47.

Chapter 6

¹Rollo May, *Love and Will* (New York: Norton, 1969), pp. 233, 234.
²Ibid., p. 234.
³Gordon Allport, *Becoming* (New Haven: Yale, 1955), p. 92.
⁴Cf. Gordon Allport, *Pattern and Growth in Personality* (New York: Holt, Rinehart and Winston, 1961), pp. 222–225.
⁵Cf. Allport, *Pattern and Growth*, p. 520.
⁶Martin Heidegger, *Being and Time* tr. John Macquarrie and Edward Robinson (London: SCM Press, 1962), p. 227.
⁷Ibid., pp. 235-241. Also see Martin Heidegger, *Existence and Being* (Chicago: Henry Regnery Co., 1949).
⁸Rollo May, p. 234.
⁹Gerald May, *Will and Spirit* (San Francisco: Harper, 1987), pp. 89, 90.
¹⁰Johannes Pedersen, *Israel: Its Life and Culture* (London: Oxford, 1926), I–II, p. 108.
¹¹Ibid.
¹²While we are staying with *nephesh*, Paul's understanding of Soul is along these same lines: an intentional vitality directed toward an end. By soul Paul means the vitality of oneself as a "striving, willing, purposing self." See Rudolf Bultmann, *Theology of the New Testament* (New York: Scribner's, 1951), tr. Kendrick Grobel, I, pp. 204–205.
¹³Pedersen, *Israel* p. 106.
¹⁴Ibid., p. 109.
¹⁵Ibid., p. 141.
¹⁶Ibid., cf. p. 108.
¹⁷Cf. John B. Cobb, Jr., *The Structure of Christian Existence* (Philadelphia: Westminster Press, 1967), ch. 10.
¹⁸Whitehead, *Religion in the Making*, p. 105.
¹⁹Ibid., pp. 119, 120.
²⁰Rom. 7—8; 2 Cor. 5:16–21; Rudolf Bultmann, *Theology of the New Testament* (New York: Scribner, 1951), I, chap. 4, passim).
²¹Meland, *The Reawakening of the Christian Faith*, p. 112.
²²James, *Varieties*, pp. 154, 255.
²³Ibid., p. 274.
²⁴*Adventures of Ideas*, p. 161.
²⁵*Process and Reality*, pp. 519, 520.
²⁶For example, see David Ray Griffin, William A. Beardslee, Joe Holland, *Varieties of Postmodern Theology* (Albany: State University of New York Press, 1989, chap. 2; and David Ray Griffin, *God and Religion in the Postmodern World* (Albany: State University of New York Press, 1989), passim.
²⁷Cf. Douglas Sturm, *Community and Alienation: Essays on Process Thought and Public Life*. Also, Robert N. Bellah et. al., *Habits of the Heart* (New York: Harper, 1986).
²⁸*Seeds of Redemption*, pp. 74–76.

122   *A Theology for Ministry*

[29] H. Richard Niebuhr, *The Purpose of the Church and Its Ministry* (New York: Harper & Row, 1956), p. 31.
[30] Ibid., pp. 32, 33.
[31] *The Cloud of Unknowing*, tr. Clifton Walters, (Penguin Books, 1961), ch. 7, passim.
[32] Carl Rogers, *Client-Centered Therapy* (Boston: Houghton Miflin, 1951), p. ix.

Chapter 7

[1] Mary Warnock, *Imagination* (Berkeley: University of California Press, 1976), p. 196.
[2] Ian J. Ramsey, *Models and Mystery* (London: Oxford University Press, 1964), p. 5.
[3] Amos Niven Wilder, *Theopoetica* (Philadelphia: Fortress Press, 1976), p. 2. Cf. science and the use of metaphor. "The images that scientists have as they do science are metaphorical. The imaginative faculties are set in motion by mental metaphor." Roald Hoffmann, Cornell University, who shared the 1981 Nobel Prize in Chemistry. (quoted in Newsweek, June 28, 1993, p. 51.)
[4] Ibid., p.12.
[5] David Bryant, *Faith and the Play of Imagination* (Macon, Ga: Mercer University Press, 1989), p. 71.
[6] Cf. Ibid., p. 77.
[7] *Ibid*, p. 87.
[8] Ibid., p. 95.
[9] Russell Kirk, "Eliot's Christian Imagination," in *The Placing of T. S. Eliot*, ed. Jewel Spears Brooker (Columbia, Mo.: University of Missouri Press, 1991), p.136.
[10] Ibid., p. 143.
[11] T. S. Eliot, *The Complete Poems and Plays, 1909–1950* (New York: Harcourt, Brace & World, 1962), pp. 4–6.
[12] Ibid., p. 108.
[13] Kirk, p. 141.
[14] Ibid., p. 136.
[15] Bernard Eugene Meland, *Seeds of Redemption*, p.56.
[16] Ibid., p. 70.
[17] Ibid., p. 70.
[18] Paul Tillich, *The Courage To Be* (New Haven: Yale University Press, 1952), p. 190.
[19] Cf. ibid., p. 188, passim.
[20] Sallie McFague, *Models of God* (Philadelphia: Fortress, 1987), chaps. 4–6.
[21] David Bryant, pp. 106f. cf., Hans-Georg Gadamer, *Truth and Method*, tr. Garrett Borden and John Cumming (New York: Continuum, 1975), pp. 73–90.
[22] Bryant, pp. 126–127.
[23] Rainier Maria Rilke, *Letters to a Young Poet*, tr. M. D. Hecter Norton (New York: Norton, 1954), Letter 3.
[24] Simone Weil, *Waiting for God*, tr. Emma Craufurd (New York: Capricorn, 1959), pp. 23, 24, 25.
[25] Meland, *Seeds*, p. 75.
[26] William James, *The Varieties of Religious Experience*, p. 254.

Chapter 8

[1] Martin Heidegger, *Existence and Being*, p. 39.
[2] Martin Heidegger, *On the Way to Language*, tr. Peter D. Hertz, (New York: Harper and Row, 1971), p. 57.
[3] *Ibid*, p. 73.
[4] Cf. Ibid, p. 74.
[5] Cf. James M. Robinson, "The German Discussion of the Later Heidegger," *The Later Heidegger and Theology* (New York: Harper and Row, VI), ed. by James M. Robinson and John B. Cobb, Jr., So Heinrich Ott focuses the human encounter with God in prayer, p.47.
[6] Ibid., p. 55.
[7] *Modes of Thought*, p. 51.
[8] Ibid., p. 52.
[9] Ibid., p. 57.
[10] Ibid.
[11] Ibid.
[12] Meland, *The Reawakening of the Christian Faith*, p. 100.
[13] Meland, *Seeds of Redemption*, p. 159.
[14] Whitehead, *Modes of Thought*, p. 229.
[15] Ibid., p. 7.
[16] Whitehead, *Adventures of Ideas*, p. 226.
[17] Whitehead, *Process and Reality*, pp. 520, 532.
[18] Huston Smith, *The Religions of Man* (New York: Mentor Books, 1958), p. 73.
[19] Ibid., p. 74.
[20] Bryant, p.161.
[21] Richard Niebuhr, *The Purpose of the Church and Its Ministry*, p. 31.
[22] Whitehead, *Adventures of Ideas*, p. 167.
[23] Martin Buber, *I and Thou* (Edinburgh: T. & T. Clark, 1937), p. 11.
[24] Cf. Ibid.
[25] Cf. Buber.
[26] Søren Kiergegaard, *Purity of Heart* tr. by Douglas V. Steere (New York: Harper & Bros., 1938), p. 177ff.
[27] Ronald Gregor Smith in Buber, *I and Thou*, p. v.
[28] Ibid., p. vii.
[29] William P. Alston, *Philosophy of Language* (Englewood Cliffs: Prentice-Hall, 1964), p. 52.
[30] Cf.Ibid., p. 65.
[31] Jackson with Jackson.
[32] Whitehead, *Adventures of Ideas*, p. 172.

Chapter 9

[1] Tillich, *Systematic Theology*, I:11,12.
[2] Ibid., p. 250.
[3] Ibid., p. 181.

4. Cf. Hartshorne, *Man's Vision of God*, p. 229.
5. Søren Kierkegaard, *Purity of Heart*, tr. by Douglas Steere (New York: Harper, 1938), passim.
6. Daniel Day Williams, *God's Grace and Man's Hope* (New York: Harper, 1949), p. 181.
7. Ibid., p.186.
8. Ibid.
9. Cf. Williams, Ibid., pp. 192 ff.
10. Whitehead, *Adventures of Ideas*, p. 167.
11. Cf. Meland, *Reawakening*, p. 92.
12. John B. Cobb, Jr., *The Structure of Christian Existence*, p. 135.
13. Cf. Reinhold Niebuhr, *The Nature and Destiny of Man*, I, chap. 7.
14. Cf. Ibid.
15. Cobb, *Structure of Christian Existence*, p. 135.
16. Lewis B. Smedes, *Forgive and Forget* (San Francisco: Harper, 1984), p. 77.
17. Erik H. Erikson, *Childhood and Society* (New York: Norton, 1950), p. 81 ff. and 222 ff.
18. Ibid., p. 83.
19. Franz Alexander, *Fundamentals of Psychoanalysis* (New York: Norton, 1963), p. 54.
20. Erikson, p. 224 ff.
21. Ibid., p. 84.
22. A. H. Maslow, *Motivation and Personality* (New York: Harper, 1954), chap. 5.
23. Erikson, *Childhood and Society*, p. 228.
24. Erik H. Erikson, *Identity Youth and Crisis* (New York: Norton, 1968), p. 130.
25. Daniel J. Levinson, *The Seasons of a Man's Life* (New York: Knopf, 1978), chaps. 14 and 15.
26. Cf. John G. Howells, ed., *Modern Perspectives in the Psychiatry of Middle Age* (New York: Burmer/Mazel, 1981), p. 15.
27. Ibid., p. 7.
28. Carl Jung, "Psychotherapists or the Clergy," in *The Collected Works*, tr. R. F. C. Hull (London: Routledge & Kegan, 1960), II, 340.
29. Carl Jung, *Modern Man in Search of a Soul* (New York: Harcourt, Brace and World, 1933), p. 61.
30. T. S. Eliot, *The Complete Poems and Plays, 1909–1950* (New York: Harcourt, Brace & World, 1962), pp. 4–6.
31. Albert Camus, *The Fall* (New York: Knopf, 1957), p. 147.
32. John B. Cobb, Jr., *The Structure of Christian Existence* (Philadelphia: Westminster, 1967), pp. 124f.
33. Arthur Cushman McGiffert, *Martin Luther The Man and His Work* (New York: Century, 1917), p. 31.
34. Whitehead, *Progress and Reality*, p.7.
35. Meland, *Seeds of Redemption*, p. 159.